YOUR
MAGIC POWERS
OF PERSUASION

Vernon Howard

No Dream Too Big Publishing
Melrose, Florida

Published by
No Dream Too Big LLC
PO Box 1220
Melrose, FL 32666   USA

www.AsAManThinketh.net

ISBN-13: 978-0-9838415-8-6

Contents

A Secret Message for You!

Here is a Special *Message* for You:
Before you start reading this book, please turn to the
section entitled *My Secret Inspirations Found in This Book.*
It can make a magical difference in your life!

—Vernon Howard

Chapter 1

YOU CAN MAGICALLY COMMAND OTHER PEOPLE

Marilyn was a pretty woman. Sitting opposite her, you could easily see that. Maybe she was even prettier in a way with her cheeks moist with tears.

With closed eyes she slowly shook her head. "Why is it," she asked, "Why is it I get into trouble?"

We sat there for a few moments without saying anything. She finally touched her handkerchief to her eyes and breathed softly, "That silence was worth far more than words. You seem to understand. Thank you."

It was easy to observe in Marilyn a truly kindly woman. She didn't ask for much. Not really. Maybe just for someone to like her a little bit and maybe for someone whom she could like in return. Take care of those two things and everything else would take care of itself. Somehow you sensed that. Here was a genuinely gracious lady.

She smiled with a shy and sweet embarrassment. "I feel better now. Could we please talk?"

"We might start directly with the problem," I suggested. "Suppose you just go ahead and chat; well take things as they come."

"I just don't understand," she said sincerely, "how a person can get into so much grief just by trying to be nice to people. I was brought up to believe in the Golden Rule, to treat others as I would want to be treated. But," she sighed, "something always seems to go wrong. Where is the fault? How have I failed?"

"Your problem, Marilyn, is typical to millions of sincere people. They fail to realize that kindness alone is not enough. Successful human relations have certain requirements: Kindness must be matched with wisdom. Love needs a measure of clear judgment. Courtesy must be joined by an understanding of the people to whom you are courteous. When you are generous you must also think clearly toward those people to whom you extend your courtesy. Otherwise you are going to get hurt."

"I don't want to complain too much," she said, "but I am tired of getting hurt. And I don't want to be afraid so much."

"Then you must understand people as they actually are, not as you wish to see them and especially as you need to see them. It's pointless to use kindness as a tool for persuading a person whose own personality makes him incapable of recognizing kindness. You have no business being tender to someone who cannot understand tenderness. You'll break your heart every time by using gentleness on a person whose immaturity prevents him from responding gently. This does not mean that we must be unkind to the unkind person; it means that we must handle him with firm wisdom."

Marilyn said she would think about these ideas until she understood them thoroughly. As soon as she does, she will open new and powerful worlds as far as her relations with other people are concerned.

Our discussion covered just one of the many basic principles which you can follow all the way to success and happiness in your dealings with other people.

Your Invisible Power

Do you remember the *Invisible Man?* No doubt you know of that classic story by H. G. Wells, seen in movies and on television. The Invisible Man had the entire world under his command because of his power to see without being seen. Because he had discovered an immense scientific secret, he exercised kingly authority. Wherever he walked among men and women he took what he wanted.

You also have an Invisible Power. It also is an immense scientific secret. It will enable you also to walk among people and obtain what you want and need for a rich and satisfying life.

Your Invisible Power is your ability to persuade and command people.

The purpose of this book is to show you how to find and how to use your Invisible Power. Once you learn the secret you will enrich every area of your life in a surprisingly delightful way. ·

Writes Professor Harry Overstreet:

We need, in short, to know how to interest our fellows; how to arouse their expectation; how to build up habits of favorable response; how to lead and adjust and control... To become skilled artists in the enterprise of life—there is hardly anything more basically needful than this.[1]

Your first step toward commanding power is to realize that everything you want is found in *other people*.

What do you want?

Money? That's a perfectly admirable ambition. But how do you get it? The only way possible. Through other people. They pay you money for your goods or your services or your labor. If you want more money you must have more influence over those who have it.

---

1   Harry Overstreet, *Influencing Human Behavior* (New York: W. W. Norton and Company, Inc., 1925).

Maybe you want more love and friendship in your life. Those necessities also mean other people. Furthermore, it means that you must know how to induce affection and cordiality in others.

Do you desire feelings of acceptance and self-worth? All right. All of us do. Other people are more than willing to contribute these valuable items to you—providing you know how to charm them rightly into doing so.

The fact is, everything we want or yearn for is won through other people. No man on an island is happy; he is merely existing. The joyous life is the one filled with rich relationships. That is why it is essential that we learn the secrets of mastering and commanding other people. Quite obviously, success of any kind is impossible as long as a man's human relations are marred by conflict or inefficiency.

No man really *wants* to be a failure among his fellow human beings.

Then why do millions fail? The answer is really quite simple: They fail to discover their Invisible Power; they neglect to use the basic secrets for wooing and winning others.

Take the lonely individual who fails to attract and keep friends. What is his real problem? Lack of people with whom to share life? Not as long as there are millions on earth. A lack of physical attractiveness? This is not the problem at all (as I will prove for you in a later chapter). I am thinking of several men and women who don't quite represent the dashing Don Juan or the ideal Venus, but who nevertheless are kept on the run by people who write them gay notes inviting, "Come to our party."

Both the lonely and those who worry about their physical appearance are allowing mistaken attitudes to rob them of personal power. In short, *they think about the wrong things.* If you want power to command other people you can have it in fantastic abundance—but you must direct your thoughts correctly. Correct thinking is that which focuses on personal power —where it is and how to get it and ways to use it. Do this and such things as loneliness and worry over physical appearance become as nothing. They really do. "Man thinks, and at once becomes the master of the beings who do not think." (Buffon)

You Can Become As Powerfully Persuasive As You Want

Recently I jokingly asked a young teen-ager, "Which of your many girl friends do you like best?"

He smiled, "Shirley."

"Why Shirley?"

"I think," he reflected with a shy grin, "it's because whenever I leave her home she keeps watching me from the front porch until I'm out of sight."

"That makes you feel good?"

"It makes me feel needed; I'm important enough to her that she wants to be with me until the last possible second. I guess you'd say that Shirley is someone special to me because she makes me feel like someone special to her."

Shirley, whoever she is, has made herself a persuasive person by the simple courtesy of filling that persistent human longing to feel needed.

Watch the exciting changes in your personal world as you practice your powers for persuading people.

Scientific studies in our universities prove clearly that those who get the most out of life are those who work accurately and smoothly with the people who surround them. That smoothly operating person can be you. The simple fact is, you can become just as powerful with other people as you make up your mind to be. So, decide right now to see yourself all the way through. Do this and nothing can prevent you from winning your magic power to command people—and getting what you want from them.

Whenever anyone asks me, "How can I learn to win my way with others?" I tell him, "Look in the right place for the power you want. Don't waste your time searching in the wrong area. Look where you should look and you will have the influence you should have."

The other day I stepped into the local library to pick up a favorite book of mine, a recreational volume telling of travel and adventure in South America. I went to the shelf where I had previously found it, only to find it missing. Thinking it had been checked out by another patron I was about to leave when I fell into conversation with the librarian. When I happened to mention the missing book she helpfully informed me, "I think you can find it after all. It has been changed to a new location." Thanks to her guidance I went to the new shelf area and immediately found the book I wanted.

Likewise, if we want personal power in our lives we can have it—providing we look in the right place.

You can learn to win your way in the world of people by looking to the proven principles and up-to-date techniques found in these pages. They are scientifically sound; they are also presented in a simple manner so that you will know just what to do.

Take, for instance, the time when you run into the shy and silent type of person. Such a man is like a cup without a handle; you can't seem to find a place to pick him up. Is there a way to handle him? There is. Just realize that his very shyness tells you what to do. He has a deep need for you to approach him, speak to him, enjoy him. Do this and you will instantly have made a loyal friend who willingly goes along with you.

That is a very brief example, but what we are saying is this: You can magically command other people because there are clear-cut ways to do it. The science of psychology has seen to that. Even if you are not presently aware of the techniques, they still exist and they always work. We will discover them together as we go through this book. Just as know-how enables an engineer to build a sturdy bridge for carrying traffic, your know-how in human relations enables you to carry loads of influence. The man who goes ahead with this fact foremost in mind is the one who gets places with people. He is the wise man, and, as Plato observed, "The wisest have the most authority."

Six Exciting Reasons Why You Should Become A Commander-In-Chief of People

Charles A. Lindbergh had a powerful desire to become the first solo pilot to fly across the Atlantic Ocean to Paris. It was that motive that pushed him all the way to history-making achievement. Noah Webster had an intense urge to collect and study words so that he could teach better grammar to his students. That motive gave Webster and his dictionary worldwide fame.

The point is this: The stronger your motive for doing anything the quicker your success. Motivation can crash through all obstacles. Here is what the book *Creative Thinking* has to say about it: "Once a goal has been selected . . . the individual must be capable of *mustering the necessary energy to carry him forward toward this goal* . . . Motivation is essential for accomplishing results in any type of endeavor."[2]

So keep yourself both motivated and enthused by remembering the following six pointers:

1. You should sharpen your talents for persuading other people because it returns to you practical rewards in the form of prestige, position, and financial security. That last item alone is reason enough for you—if you are at all interested in money! Chapter 12 shows you how to persuade your way to financial increase.

2. The power to influence is a power for good, or as author George Eliot called it, the blessed influence of one true loving soul on another." The parent who masters the art of tactfully persuading his children and the employer who guides his employees with skill and diplomacy are certainly worthy forces for making life easier and happier. The maturely influential person is valuable to himself and to his family and to his community.

---

2   Charles S. Whiting, Creative Thinking (New York: Reinhold Publishing Corporation, 1958).

3. Power with people keeps you out of trouble with people. Most problems a man has with other people are avoidable, providing you know what to avoid. Back in 1890, a bird-lover imported several pairs of starlings from England to New York City. They quickly multiplied until they became serious threats to farm crops. Had the United States Government realized the destructiveness of these birds they would have forbidden them entrance in the first place. Likewise do you need to recognize and handle people who could become a problem to you. (Chapters 3 and 8 go into detail about this.)

4. Personal power gives you a sense of accomplishment. It enables you to live fully and zestfully. It provides you with a mature reason for liking yourself better. To state it another way, it is the mark of a healthy and well-adjusted individual to seek self-advancement by mastering his human relations.

5. You should become a commander-in-chief of people be-cause it keeps you relaxed and peaceful in your daily living.

    The other day while driving my car I came to a red light just as a police car sped toward me from the opposite direction. The police car was still heading my way as the signal turned green, so in requirement to law I remained in place. The man in the car behind me suddenly pounded his horn and annoyedly gestured for me to get going. Now there was a circumstance which might easily have bothered me, but I was able to think to myself, "He just doesn't understand. He doesn't see the police car." A moment later, when he did understand the situation, he grinned and threw me an apologetic wave of his hand.

    That illustrates how an understanding of people not only saves wear and tear on the nervous system, but wins the other man over to your side. When you really understand the human processes at work in any given situation, you give yourself power for peace in that situation.

6. Finally, it's fun to win your way! (As if you didn't know!) There is every reason why you should make it an exciting challenge to see how skillfully you can handle people. It's a challenge that can return immense benefits.

Go After Clear-cut Goals

Make it absolutely clear to yourself *what you want* from other people. That is really half the secret for drawing your desire to you in the shortest possible time and with the least amount of effort. Dr. Rollo May writes in his book *Mans Search for Himself*:

> The mark of the mature man is that his living is integrated around self-chosen goals: he knows what he wants, no longer simply as the child wants ice cream but as the grown person plans and works toward a creative love relationship or toward business achievement or what not.[3]

In other words, establish a definite purpose in your contacts with people, for it is a fact that "Purpose directs energy, and purpose makes energy." (C. H. Parkhurst)

Do it like this: Read carefully the goals and objectives listed below. While all of them are good for you it is best that you select just those five goals which are most important to you as of today. So select your five, then write the numbers, 1, 2, 3, 4, 5 after them in order of their importance to you. You now have five clearly defined objectives. Keep yourself reminded (and enthused!) by reviewing them every time you have the opportunity to do so; better yet, make the opportunity to impress yourself with what you want. Just as a hunter needs to peer at his quarry before he can take proper aim, so do you need to look over your objectives before firing away at them with the techniques found in this book.

---

3   Rollo May, Ph.D., *Mans Search for Himself* (New York: W. W. Norton and Company, Inc., 1953).

Apply the various techniques to your first five goals, then when you have attained them, select and go to work on five more. Swiss author Henri Amiel once declared that "Order is power." Well, here is the orderly way to win the power you want.

My Present Five Goals Are to:

1. Win a certain person to my way of thinking.

2. Make myself interesting to people.

3. Make myself understood by others.

4. Win a career promotion.

5. Get others to recommend and promote me.

6. Handle everyone with maximum skill.

7. Stop being afraid of people.

8. Solve a definite problem with someone.

9. Be natural when with people.

10. Sell more of my goods or services.

11. Draw more friendliness and affection.

12. Banish loneliness.

13. Let others feel comfortable with me.

14. Attract favorable attention.

15. Be more attractive to the opposite sex.

16. Feel less frustrated.

17. Win cooperation from others.

18. Be more patient with difficult people.

19. Influence my family in a beneficial way.

20. Take instant charge of a human situation.

21. Persuade others quickly and effortlessly.

22. Influence others to seek me out.

23. Feel less threatened by people.

24. Be more relaxed on social occasions.

25. Talk my way into what I want.

26. Establish peaceful relations.

27. Attract more customers and clients.

28. Be firm and positive when with others.

29. Command others wisely and tactfully.

30. Get others to do things for me.

31. Stay out of trouble.

32. Regain the friendship of a particular person.

33. Be clever in going after what I want.

34. Earn more money.

35. Persuade another to obey my reasonable requests.

36. Really understand the ways of human nature.

37. Bounce back instantly when thwarted by someone.

38. Be more popular.

39. Allow my feelings to be hurt less often.

40. Induce a certain person to be kinder to me.

Maybe you have some special and personal areas where you wish to sharpen your effectiveness with people. Write them down below; add them to your program.

1. _____

2. _____

3. _____

4. _____

5. _____

6. _____

7. _____

8. _____

9. _____

10. _____

Here is how one alert businessman selected and worked with a clear-cut objective. He chose goal 34, which reads, "Earn more money."

He made up his mind to increase the persuasiveness of his newspaper advertisements. After thinking things through he sat down and prepared the text of his new advertisement. It started off with large and bold words which asked: WANT A DIAMOND TO LAND IN YOUR FRONT YARD? IT COULD HAPPEN TODAY!

Talk about persuasiveness! Everyone who read those captivating words were compelled to read on. As they did so, they heard the exciting story about Dr. G. A. Koenig of the Museum of Natural History of New York.

> Dr. Koenig was exploring a rugged canyon in Arizona when he ran across that most fabulous of all gems, a diamond. To find a natural diamond in the United States was sensational enough in itself, but it was still only a fraction of the fantastic story. The gem was imbedded in a meteorite! Here was a diamond from outer space!
>
> The advertisement then went on to suggest that the reader himself just might be visited by sparkling fortune, for who knows when another diamond from another world might plunge into his front yard. The advertisement then went on to tell of the "diamond-like products" to be found at the merchant's store.
>
> That businessman knew a few things about persuading people. His advertisement started off with a mystifying statement that caught immediate attention. It promised the reader personal gain. It told an exciting story that really happened.
>
> By starting with his definite goal to earn more money, that businessman helped himself to follow through with a practical plan for influencing more people to buy his goods. And this they did!

One of the headline principles you should remember in all your dealings with people is:

Everyone Wants and Needs Persuasion

I am thinking of a psychologist whose accomplishments in both the world of business and in social affairs entitle him to the rank of expert.

> As a classroom instructor he has his own special system for turning timid businessmen and shy homemakers into capable people-persuaders. One of his techniques is to take a student to the window of the classroom where he asks him to look out-

side. As the student does so, the conversation goes something like this:

"See that woman getting out of her car?" asks the instructor.

"Yes."

"How did she get that car?"

"Someone sold it to her."

"How come she's wearing a wristwatch?"

"She was persuaded that it was the right one for her."

"Where did she get that attractive pair of shoes?"

"From a salesman."

"Why do you suppose she wears that particular hair-style?"

"Someone guided her in selecting it."

"She's meeting that man on the corner. How come?"

"He invited her to meet him there."

The dialogue goes on until the point is thoroughly driven home. And what is the point? Just this: *Everyone constantly needs and looks for persuasion and guidance from others.* As a matter of fact, life would be impossible without the power of influence. The school teacher guides her pupils toward knowledge, the salesman persuades his customers to buy his goods, the clergyman exerts influence toward loftier living. All this is fairly obvious, but you may need to realize fully that the dependencies and needs of others are your opportunities for worthy leadership. Another way of saying this is that we all have hundreds of needs that require the influential services of another. In the pages of this book you will learn about hundreds of these basic needs which, when fulfilled in another by you, make you a welcome influence.

Dr. Sidney M. Jourard expresses the idea like this:

Thus the most effective means of inducing change in the other person is to behave toward him in ways which will satisfy his basic needs. Then, the wishes of the first person, within reason . . . will literally become the other person's willingly obeyed commands.[4]

We need to act toward the other person so that he or she *wants* to please us. That is the secret. This is excellently illustrated by the deeply-loved lady who asked her man, "Why are you so nice to me?"

"Because, dear," he tenderly explained, "you make me *want* to be nice to you."

People appreciate and follow the person who can persuade them properly. Make that person you.

---

4   Sidney M. Jourard, *Personal Adjustment* (New York: The Macmillan Company, 1958). Reprinted by permission of the publishers.

Review Your First Commanding Steps

1. Remember that your skill in human relations is an invisible and just about irresistible power. It wins astonishing success for you wherever you want.

2. It is a fact that all you want and need for the happy life is found with and through other people.

3. Remember that there are no real barriers to prevent you from attaining the magic power to persuade and command people; there are only negative attitudes. This book supplies the system for dissolving them.

4. Failure becomes an impossibility to the man who knows how to win people.

5. How powerful do you want to become? That, really, is how powerful you can be. All you need do is start, with or without self-confidence. Just start.

6. Remember that throughout these pages you are working with scientifically-proven principles. They work. Let them work for you.

7. There is a sure way to handle and win every type of person in your life. Employ the right system and you win every time.

8. Keep yourself excited about becoming a persuasive per son. Remind yourself constantly of all the benefits.

9. Discover exactly what you want. Don't hesitate to tell yourself about it every day. This simple act releases extra energy for driving you toward your goal.

10. Realize the tremendous need that other people have for the strong and persuasive personality. Make yourself that kind of personality and you magically enrich your life.

Chapter

START RIGHT NOW TO WIN YOUR WAY WITH OTHERS

During the Third Crusade of the Middle Ages, the English knights under Richard the Lion-Hearted ran into a problem. The problem was built of stone. It was a massive, strongly fortified castle held by the fierce and fanatical Turks. The Crusaders knew that the castle had to be captured if the crusade was to push on to its final objective in the Holy Land.

King Richard directed a frontal attack by handpicked infantry-men against the main gate. The soldiers were driven back with staggering losses. A desperate charge by the English cavalry was also beaten back with heavy casualties. A third assault by a combined force of archers and crossbowmen failed utterly; the main gate stood firm.

It looked as if King Richard's plan to march on to the conquest of the Holy Land was defeated, or at the very best, stalled for months to come.

But Richard wasn't called the Lion-Hearted for nothing. If the castle couldn't be taken by frontal assault, there must be an-other way—and the King was determined to find it.

One evening the English monarch had a group of prisoners brought in for questioning. A Turkish bowman let slip the information that the castle was undermined by a series of secret passages leading from the stronghold to concealed exits in the surrounding woods. That very night the Crusaders slipped down into the openings and silently raced along the hidden tunnels. Within ten minutes they penetrated beyond the overhead walls, and inside another five minutes they burst out into the castle itself, with swishing swords. The surprised and overwhelmed Turks surrendered almost without a struggle. The castle fell. King Richard and his legions marched triumphantly through the main gate.

This illustrates much more than a successful military tactic; it is a sound principle that you can employ with considerable triumph in your march toward winning others.

As we saw in Chapter 1, people are quite willing to be persuaded by you, but you must use the "secret passages" to get to them.

Henry Clay Lindgren observes:

One of the facts of human relations which we must learn again and again... is that there are better and more effective ways of supervising people than through the use of direct force. Indeed, the really successful leader is one who does not have to use force at all in order to carry out his functions as a leader.[5]

The direct approach usually fails because it arouses fear in the other person that you are trying to dominate him or put one over on him. Of course the people you wish to win are not your enemies, but even the friendliest of friends will stiffen their defenses against a slam-bang attack. When you approach another with techniques that boldly

---

5   Reprinted from *The Art of Human Relations*, copyright 1953, by Henry Clay Lindgren, Thomas Nelson & Sons, Publishers.

broadcast, "I'm going to win you over," his natural self-defensiveness is sure to counterattack with, "That's what you think."

Bear in mind:

> A man takes contradiction and advice much more easily than people think, only he will not bear it when violently given, even though it be well founded. Hearts are flowers, they remain open to the soft-falling dew, but shut up in the violent downpour of rain. (Ritcher)

Women especially resent the blunt approach when being persuaded to buy this or agree to that. They don't mind being won, but they prefer a little wooing first.

Besides, when you make your point of attack too obvious you enable the other man to concentrate all his resources against it. That often results in a stalemate with no one winning and everyone losing. Another thing you should remember is this: Whenever anyone knows that you desperately want something from him he tends to withhold it, for it gives him a very satisfying sense of power over you. He knows that as long as he keeps you at bay that you will continue to seek him out. That gives him a great sense of self-importance that he won't easily give up. Your indifferent attitude is sometimes far more effective than might be imagined.

Inasmuch as the blunt approach defeats itself far too often, what are the alternatives, what are the "secret passages" that lead you to your conquest? You will find dozens of them explained in these pages, but one of the primary rules to remember is that:

Self-interest is Everyone's First Interest

The story is told of a fellow named Tom who came to his best friend Harry for some advice on a love affair:

> "Harry, I can marry a wealthy lady who doesn't excite me at all, or I can wed a poor girl whom I love passionately. Which one should I choose?"

"By all means," his friend quickly replied, "be true to your heart-felt passion and marry the girl you love. And by the way," the friend slyly added, "give me the name of the wealthy one."

This is the humorous way of pointing out that when all is said and done, self-interest comes before any other interest. Everyone tends to see things according to his private needs and desires. We interpret and we act for our personal benefits. That is the plain fact about human nature and that is what you must work with if you are to influence it. Nature made us that way for the sake of survival. Remember that constructive self-interest is *not* the same thing as selfishness. The selfish person's very selfishness prevents him from serving his own best welfare. Generosity is a result of knowing how to serve yourself so well that your very abundance of happiness makes it possible for you to let it overflow onto others. Here is how Dr. Sandor S. Feldman sums it up: "We think first of ourselves. Only when we are taken care of can we afford to think of the other fellow."[6]

After discussing the foregoing ideas with me, Glen K., an accountant, came up with this question: "But if self-interest is a man's primary interest, where does that leave me, I mean, how can I get him interested in me?"

"It's really very easy," I told him, "once you understand what you must do."

"What must I do to sell myself to the other man?"

"Sell him on himself. That is what you must remember first, last, and always. This doesn't mean you have to indulge in idle flattery or anything else so shallow; it merely means that you assist him in living up to the kind of person he wants to be. Everyone has doubts about his ability to become a better person; by as-

---

6   Sandor S. Feldman, M.D., *Mannerisms of Speech and Gestures in Everyday Life* (New York: International Universities Press, Inc., 1959).

suring him that he isn't doing so badly you attract his attention and his approval."

Glen said he would concentrate on this pointer. As he does so, he will see how easy it is to turn the other man's self-interest into mutual profit.

In what areas does a man like to be sold on himself? There are hundreds of areas where you can help to build a man's "Picture-preference." By this term we mean that every man has a picture of himself as he prefers to see himself. (Psychiatrists like Dr. Freud call it *self-image* or *self-concept*.) It is no surprise that his Picture-preference is a complimentary one; there is no man on earth who doesn't prefer to think of himself as being bright rather than dull, or powerful rather than weak.

You become a creative artist in human relations by contributing to another's Picture-preference. Let's look at some of them.

People prefer to appear:	*And prefer not to appear:*
1. to be sought-after	*to be ignored.*
2. to be clever	*to be witless.*
3. to be someone special	*to be one of the crowd.*
4. to be daring	*to be timid.*
5. to be an exciting person	*to be dull.*
6. to be discerning	*to be gullible.*
7. to be energetic	*to be a rash thinker.*
8. to be needed	*to be unwanted.*
9. to be self-sufficient	*to be weak.*

10. to be relaxed   *to be tense.*

11. to be modest   *to be vain.*

12. to be on the way up   *to be futureless.*

13. to be courteous   *to be impolite.*

14. to be mature   *to be childish.*

Give yourself some practical practice at this point by writing down five of your personal Picture-preferences. Since we all like pretty much the same things, you can be sure that others will want them also. Now you have five more ideas for selling a man on himself—and also on you.

People prefer to appear: *And prefer not to appear:*

1._____   _____

2._____   _____

3._____   _____

4._____   _____

5._____   _____

You Can Make a Habit of Winning Others

You can start right now to win your way with others by remembering, "Habit is the deepest law of human nature." (Carlyle) Also, "Habit is necessary to give power." (Hazlitt)

Have you ever noticed how some people have the happy habit of being charming and interesting persons? You like them instinctively and you have the feeling that they like you also. And also notice how others habitually fail to attract either attention or admiration? You just can't warm up to them.

No doubt you realize that habit is a powerful and persistent characteristic of human nature. Better yet, let's identify it as **a** helpful and necessary servant, for that is what a positive habit really is. Because you have established the habit of eating breakfast in a certain manner you can also turn your mind to the morning newspaper. Your habit of walking down the street is so well established as a subconsciously directed process that you can also toss around in your mind your various business affairs. Habit makes things simple and efficient. That much is obvious.

Because of all this, habit is too tremendous a force to ignore when it comes to human relations. The wise man throws it into the battle for advancing his aims. That is why I next want to show you how to turn the force of habit into a power for commanding and winning other people to your way. It works magic for the person who works with it.

Now, then, it is a well-known psychological law that a habit is formed through pleasurable repetition. The first time we tasted candy we liked the taste. Because we wanted to continue the pleasure we repeated the tasting. This established the pleasant habit of enjoying candy. It is something we like to be associated with constantly.

The very same principle applies in a person-to-person relationship. Someone meets you and you offer him a pleasant smile. Because he likes to be smiled at, he goes away with a warm memory of your smile. The next time you meet him perhaps you say something complimentary about him. Your compliment reinforces the warmth already generated by the previous smile. He enjoys thoroughly the pleasurable sensation-upon-pleasurable sensation. The third time you meet, ask him to tell you about himself. This adds a third pleasure to the first two. About this time his mind gratefully asks, "Why do I feel so good?" Another part of his mind replies, "Because of the *person* who supplies you with your warm feelings." He now associates you with his pleasant feeling of self-esteem. His liking for himself overflows into a liking for you. He can't help but be attracted to the author of his pleasure.

Furthermore, because he likes you he will want to please you. So that you will continue to supply him with pleasurable feelings, he will do whatever he can to supply you with the same. (Here we see at work the familiar law of give and take.)

Summary: Your repeated pleasantries will induce the other person to habitually yield to you the very best that he or she possesses. By this means you can build a habit of winning others the effortless way.

One way to establish yourself as a repeated winner in your human relations is to:

Return Again And Again To The Basic Principles
Governing Human Nature.

Stonewall Jackson, the brilliant Confederate commander who won victory after victory over the Northern armies, was sitting on a log one afternoon reading a small book. He was noticed by a pair of young lieutenants who were rushing toward the front lines where a battle was about to explode.

"The general sits there calmly reading a book just as we're about to attack the enemy," puzzledly gasped one of the young officers. "It's hard to understand how he always whips the Yankees."

"If you knew the book he is reading," explained the other, "you would know why he always wins."

What was the book that so absorbed General Jackson? It was one that he carried with him and referred to constantly—the *Military*

Maxims of Napoleon. Jackson had the wisdom to persistently study and review the basic rules of warfare as laid down by the French emperor.

What has this to do with you and the winning of your personal campaigns with people? It will help you to remember that there is no such thing as knowing all there is to know about engaging and winning people. You must continually seek to understand why and how people behave as they do, for "Whatever you cannot understand you cannot possess." (Goethe) The campaign requires constant additions to your know-how. Knowledge piled upon knowledge gives you power upon power.

Let's take two examples:

Curtis H., a land developer, instituted a program which offered free tours of the countryside to prospective real estate investors. In his mailings he urged the prospects to phone his office to make the arrangements for the trips. Because he was a careful student of human behavior he was curious to discover if there was a pattern of some sort covering those who phoned in and those who did not. He discovered there was. Far fewer calls came from those who had to make a toll call in order to reach his office. Curtis promptly removed that block by making arrangements to pay for the calls himself. It cost him a few extra dollars per month in his phone bill—and it earned him several hundred dollars per month in additional business.

Remember that removing a minor block in the other person's way may lead to that person making a major decision in your favor.

Paul K., a newly appointed junior executive in a cosmetics firm, was assigned the task of planning the company's annual picnic. Since time was short he needed a female assistant who could help him to get things done in a hurry. His problem was that he had his choice of more than 30 ladies around the office, none of whom he knew very well. Paul recalled a psychological principle that goes like this: "People who are quick and brisk in their physical movements are quite likely to be efficient and decisive. Their physical quickness is an extension of their mental alertness." By keeping his eyes open Paul soon found the efficient assistant he needed.

Anyone else could have done likewise, for you can gather all sorts of useful information about people just by watching their physical movements, such as the way they walk and gesture. Dr. Sandor S. Feldman points out, "Every human being has his own particular gait through which he can be characterized and recognized."[7]

People who fail to get places with other people are like the little boy who kept falling out of bed at night. When his mother asked him why it always happened he shrugged his reply, "I guess it's because I stay too near the place where I got in."

You need not fall out in your relations with others. *Not* if you will persistently go beyond whatever knowledge about people you now possess. *Not* if you will assume that there is always lots more to learn. There always is. "Victory," declared Napoleon, "belongs to the most persevering."

The rest of this chapter is devoted to some of the basic principles which you should habitually employ.

General Rules for Specific Successes

1. TURN THEIR MISTAKES INTO YOUR PROFIT

People are forever making mistakes in your favor. Get to know what they are. When a man becomes angry at you he is telling you that he fears your strength. When a person sullenly withdraws from you he is informing you how much you really mean to him. Always go beyond the act to find the real motive (which is usually not the same motive he informs you of). Never take another's explanation of his behavior at face value; he may be trying to save face. Always use

---

7   Sandor S. Feldman, M.D., *Mannerisms of Speech and Gestures in Everyday Life* (New York: International Universities Press, Inc., 1959).

another's mistakes toward you as a tool for winning him over or for building your personal strength.

As an example of how you can use others to build your personal powers:

> A married couple were imposed upon by thoughtless relatives who constantly invaded their privacy and wasted their time. After studying the situation they told the relatives, "We are cutting down on our social hours. Too much else we want to do. We'll get together when we can." The relatives reacted with surprise and injured pride—but they also responded in the way that thoughtless people will always react to polite strength —with respect. That married couple wisely used that problem-situation to add more independence to their lives.

2. ENCOURAGE PEOPLE TO EXPRESS THEIR SECRET FEELINGS

People are far more extreme in emotional make-up than appears on the surface. They are capable of far more affection than they dare to show and are also able to act with more hostility than they want others to know about. They behave with outward moderation because they want you to think they are in control of themselves. Everyone wants desperately to express both their positive and negative urges. They hesitate to let themselves go because they think they may open themselves to criticism or because they fear it may be socially unacceptable or because they want to maintain a certain pose.

You become a persuasive personality as you permit others to release both their secret affections and their hostilities. They deeply appreciate someone who can hear of these secret emotions without being shocked by them.

> A woman once told me she wanted to ignite an outward show of affection between herself and her utterly bashful boy friend. Yet she didn't want to seem to be a bold woman. I advised, "The next time you walk down the street together slip your arm under his and clutch clingingly. That is a perfectly natural action

on your part and one that will make him feel needed by you. Keep doing that and he will get the idea that you like him. That should encourage him to start a few things on his own."

Another woman told me she was troubled by daily headaches. I asked her whom she hated. As soon as she got over the shock of seeing her hostility (for one of her relatives) brought out into the open, she thanked me profusely. She said, "What a relief to find someone who lets me be hateful without condemning me for it."

Permit people to reveal themselves to you fully and freely.

3. "WHAT A POWER THERE IS IN INNOCENCE!" (Moore)

There is nothing like innocence and naturalness for persuading people to do what you want them to do. If you don't think so, just watch what happens when some wide-eyed and curly-topped little girl snuggles up to dad and asks him for something. Dad doesn't stand a chance.

A simple and direct request for whatever you want has a disarming charm all its own. People are so tired of guile and trickery that it comes as a cool breeze on a hot day when they meet someone whose persuasion comes from an innocent personality.

By innocence we don't mean weakness or gullibility or anything like that. A man doesn't have to be weak to be innocent; he merely has to be a real person. People somehow sense that there is a great deal of strength in the man who can lay aside all artificiality and be himself, regardless of what that self might be. This kind of strength has enormous appeal, for we like to see in others what we would like to see in ourselves.

4. BE REALISTIC RATHER THAN IDEALISTIC ABOUT PEOPLE

Don't idealize people. Most of us do this to a wider extent than we may think. We lose the power to understand other people when we see them according to the way we need or want to see them. If a person has a deep need for people to be kindly toward him, he will tend to expect others to be kindly; that is what he will look for. But if the facts eventually contradict the ideal, then that person will become disappointed and perhaps bitter.

This does not mean that you have to go to the other extreme of suspecting others of unkind motives. It means that you do not draw your personal picture of another as you would like him to be, but rather you let him draw his own picture of himself in his own due time. Let other people be whatever they really are and you will not be disappointed in them. You are disappointed only when the real doesn't match the ideal.

Maybe you ask, "But shouldn't I think the very best of everyone?" The answer is, you can only really think the best of everyone when you *do* see them as they really are—with all their virtues and all their shortcomings. Any other viewpoint indicates resistance to the realities about people, and in that there is plenty of pain.

Besides—and this is of utmost significance to you—people always respond to your persuasions according to their real nature, not according to any idealistic ideas you may have about them. Hit them where they really live and you'll win them over.

5. FIND SOMETHING RIGHT IN EVERYTHING THAT SEEMS WRONG

You can find something of value in everything that happens to you. This is one of those truisms that everyone likes to believe but has trouble with when it comes to putting it into practice.

The chief problem which most people have—it may be your problem also—is that they resist a negative event instead of trying to understand it.

Never fight a disappointment which people may bring into your life, rather, look out for something which you can use for your growth. The enrichment is always there. But you have to make up your mind that you will find it. Do so and you will.

Not to learn from experience is to pay the price without getting the product.

One man, now an executive in the electronics industry, told me this during a dinner conversation:

> Once, as a young salesman, I called on a prospect whom I thought would welcome me and my goods with open arms. From someplace I had gotten the idea that he desperately needed my products. Then, to my utter shock, he turned me down completely. Walking down the street I got to thinking about it. The more I thought about it the happier I got. Here is why: I got to thinking that if a *likely* prospect would say *no*, there must also be some *unlikely* prospects who might say *yes*. That would seem to be some sort of a law of averages that I could use. I decided to test it by calling on several prospects who had been on my unlikely list. I gave them a highly enthusiastic sales presentation, and was again shocked— they bought twice as much as I had hoped for! Since then I have never failed to remember that a turn-down can always be used in some way as a turn-up. Incidentally, I later went back and sold a sizeable order to the very man who, by turning me down, had given my sales career a sharp boost.

Summary: Find something right with everything that seems wrong.

6. A WAY TO SWAY

Here is a good way to remember the four principles which form the foundation of all your programs of persuasion:

a. Let them *See*. This means that you bring your program or product or idea to their attention.

b. Make them *Want*. In this step you show them how your program will enrich them in some way.

c. Lead them to *Agree*. At this point you guide them into positive responses to your idea.

d. Persuade them to *Yield*. You get them to take the final step, such as signing for your products or adopting your viewpoint.

Notice that the first letters in these key words spell SWAY. Remember SWAY and you will sway people to your way.

7. AVOID THE APPEARANCE OF BEING A THREAT

Once I was watching a class of polka dancers composed of about 50 men and women who had taken up the recreation for the first time. All of a sudden, in the middle of one of the dances, the instructor cut off the music and snapped into the microphone with a grim manner, "You've got to pay more attention if you want to get things right." Those few words spoken in a critical spirit promptly ruined that man as a popular instructor. He may have been right in what he had to say, but no one appreciated the tactless way he said it. In other words, his attitude was unnecessarily threatening.

People are tremendously sensitive, hence easily frightened and dismayed by faultfinding from others. Even when people don't show it on the surface they react strongly to the words and acts and facial expressions of those with whom they associate. This is especially true when something seems to threaten their self-esteem. All of us tend to withdraw from the person who damages our feelings of self-worth.

Remember the sensitivity of people. Take care to avoid all appearance of being a threat to their self-esteem.

Secrets for Exerting Instant Influence

1. Don't use a frontal attack when trying to change some one. Use the secret passages.

2. Remember that self-interest is everyone's first interest. Satisfy the wants of the other person and you influence that person toward satisfying your own.

3. Contribute to the Picture-preference of the other man. He needs your assurance that he is liked and welcomed. This is a forceful influence in your behalf.

4. Employ the power of habit in all your people-persuading programs. It saves time and effort.

5. Study constantly the principles governing human behavior. They are your tools for winning success-through-people. But take it easy; don't try to understand everything at once. Things will get much clearer as you proceed.

6. Never permit another's mistake to upset you. Always use it to strengthen your position.

7. Let the other man express and release his secret feelings to you. When he does so, do not react with surprise or shock or criticism; he will appreciate you as you simply understand and accept him.

8. Try the simple and direct request for what you want. It has a quiet charm all its own.

9. If you want to influence people with maximum force, see them as they really are, not as they appear to be on the surface of their personalities. People respond to persuasion according to their real natures.

10. Remember the extreme sensitivity of people. Let them be sensitive to your kindness and to your strength.

CLEARING YOUR PATH TOWARD COMMANDING POWER

In high school we used to have a teacher who customarily greeted a new class by printing the following on the blackboard:

PRO-SPE-RI-TY

She would then ask us to pronounce the well-known word spelled by those letters. After letting the mystery build up for a moment she solved it by removing the hyphens. On second look the letters come out:

PROSPERITY

She then went into her opening lesson which might be summed up like this:

At the start of any new program, be sure that you search out all blocks and obstacles. Work at removing them. Everything else will then fall into place quite easily. That is the logical and intelligent way to find your personal prosperity.

I have found one fact to be outstandingly clear about people who consult me about their problems: They have certain blocks which separate them from prosperous human relations. So the purpose of this chapter is to search out and remove some of the barriers which might stand in the way. It is delightfully surprising how the correction of a single false viewpoint can instantly make right dozens of things that may now hamper your progress. Take the following commonly held idea about human motivation: Most people think they guide themselves with practical and unemotional thinking.   But do they?

> One builder of private swimming pools thought so. That's why his advertising stressed low-cost construction and economical maintenance. When his salesman continued to come back with only a handful of contracts he wondered what was wrong with his advertising. He consulted an expert in the field who informed him: "People are persuaded largely by their emotions, not by their logic." That builder's advertising now succeeds, for it appeals to a man's pride of ownership and to his imagination which allows him to see himself lazily floating in a luxurious pool of water.

Are You Taking Enough?

Winning your way with other people is just as much an art as painting a landscape or playing a musical composition. And like these creative processes, it is a highly appreciated art. The strong leader never has to look far for loyal followers.

Leadership is a creative art which you can develop with increasing skill as you go along.

However, there is a certain mental barrier which can block this creative process unless you hurdle it at the very start. What is it? Just this:

You must freely and cheerfully admit that you want and need things from other people.

All of us do want various items from others, yet some people feel subconsciously that there is something wrong about it. Such an attitude is based on mistaken notions concerning relations with other people. Let's clarify things:

Life exists on a give-and-take basis. Our parents and teachers encouraged us to *give* of ourselves—which is as it should be—but at the same time it is equally vital to our health and welfare that we learn how to *take*. *You need to receive just as much as you need to give.* It has long been known by psychologists and therapists that people who have the ability to receive love are the happiest kind of people, and, of course, they are the only ones who can give love in return. To the degree that you can take freely, to that same degree can you give freely—and vice versa. This is an enormously important idea to grasp, for it means everything in your quest for personal power.

> Take Arnold L. who admitted to a serious problem. He not only had difficulty in getting others to cooperate with him but frequently found himself lacking the ability to work harmoniously with others. He told me, "I try to be a giver and all that, but somehow I always end up unhappy about it. I give up"
>
> "Good," I congratulated him. "Now that you see the futility of the wrong approach, you can go ahead with the right one."
>
> He tilted his head to ask curiously, "What's the right approach?"
>
> "Go at it from the opposite end. Don't give for a while. Deliberately set out to get as much as you can from people. You should do this cheerfully and without the slightest feeling of guilt about it. This is really what you want to do anyway; don't try to hide your desires under some cloak of sentimental nonsense having no relation to realistic living. We are trying to free you from yourself. Simply receive as much as you can. This isn't greediness or anything like that. Giving and getting is neither good nor bad, it is simply a neutral law of life. Cooperate with both parts and you'll have the wholeness you want. Lay yourself wide open to everything you can receive from people."
>
> "Like what?"

"Like whatever you really want. Like taking the initiative in establishing a profitable relationship. Like permitting yourself to enjoy fully another's company without being afraid of him. Like letting others do things for you without you feeling there is something wrong about being served."

"Funny," Arnold said, "but it's a relief to hear you say that.   I feel a kind of freedom I've never sensed before."

"You are in conflict with other people because you are first of all in conflict with yourself. For instance, at some time or other in your life you were told that it is right and proper to be a generous person. But not quite knowing what was meant by being a generous person you adopted a non-realistic ideal about generosity. Consequently, every time you acted with that false kind of generosity, you secretly resented it—especially when it wasn't returned by the other person."

He nodded. "I've often wondered where my bitterness came from."

"To repeat, use the opposite approach. Start taking. Deliberately and cheerfully. Without thinking too much about it. Pretty soon you will be surprisingly free from your false notions as to what life is really all about. Then you will find yourself a truly spontaneous giver. Then you will get along with people as you really want to get along."

"This may be the answer I've been searching for."

"It is."

Summary and review: All of the foregoing ideas are so vital to your progress that I want to review them with you before we go on.

You must fully and freely acknowledge that you want and need what other people have. Then, you must have the courage to step up and take whatever you want. It might be their friendship or their assistance or anything else. By doing so you are only being honest with your own desires, and that is both commendable and healthy. You must not hesitate to give *and* take. It is a universal law that you can take only as you give, so in your very taking you are giving to another. Therefore the fulfillment of your desires is not only essential to your own success and happiness but it contributes to the welfare of others.

Listen to what Dr. Ernest Dichter has to say:

Creativity can be engendered and developed if we train ourselves not to be afraid of our own thoughts. Utter honesty and understanding of one's real motivations as far as this is possible are requirements for such an achievement ... To associate freely, therefore, and permit almost all your thoughts to come out into the open either for yourself or in discussions is one of the prime prerequisites for the development of creativity.[8]

By frankly conceding "I want something," you set in motion a powerful drive that gets that something for you. So do it now. You are now ready for the next step in clearing your path toward commanding power.

How to Avoid Problems With People in the First Place

Some months ago when I was being escorted through a cookie factory I saw an excellent example of an artist in human relations. My guide and I passed within a short distance of a pair of employees who were nearing a minor conflict with each other. Their disagreement was apparently based on a division of duties in loading a truck, for one of them complained to the other, "It's not my job to help you load; you'll have to do it by yourself."

The other man nodded pleasantly and replied casually, "As you wish." He then started to work alone. But a moment later the

---

8   Ernest Dichter, *The Strategy of Desire* (New York: Doubleday and Company, Inc., 1960). Reprinted by permission of the publisher.

other man stepped over, handed him a box, grinned and said, "I'll give you a hand for a few minutes at least. Okay?"

Actually, both those men deserve credit. The man who calmly proceeded with the task on hand was wise in refusing to create a problem in the first place. He had the good sense to place his peace of mind above his urge to fling back a curt remark. By using the principle of non-aggression he won first of all a personal victory within himself, then proceeded to attract the cooperation of the other man. He was skillful enough to know that nothing calms down an uncooperative person more than quiet agreement.

As for the other man, he had at least the goodness to bounce back from his irritability. Whether it was or was not his duty to load the truck was beside the point; the point was his responsibility for handling the situation with smoothness and tact. Failing in this at first, he made the correction which made friends.

Nothing proves your intelligence more than the ability to avoid problems with people in the first place. Furthermore, the fewer your problems the brighter your personality. As Dr. Karen Horney writes, "... a conflict that starts with our relation to others in time affects the whole personality. Human relationships are so crucial that they are bound to mold the qualities we develop, the goals we set for ourselves, the values we believe in."[9]

That is why the following check list is of daily value. The questions are short but none is slight. Every one of them has significance. Write *yes* after as many as you honestly can. Answer *no* to all the rest, then make up your mind that you are so tired of having trouble with people that you will work to turn every *no* into a *yes*.

1. Do I try to understand a difficult situation?   _____

2. Am I freeing myself of defensive attitudes?   _____

3. Do I permit others to be comfortable with me?   _____

9   Karen Horney, M.D., *Our Inner Conflicts* (New York: W. W. Norton and Company, Inc., 1945).

4. Do I look for solutions instead of scapegoats?   _____

5. Am I actually willing to improve myself?   _____

6. Do I permit myself to have fun with people?   _____

7. Am I avoiding self-righteousness?   _____

8. Do I experiment constantly in winning my way?   _____

9. Do I strive to win by non-offensive means?   _____

10. Do I refuse to be easily offended?   _____

11. Am I making it easy for others to like me?   _____

12. Do I maintain inviting attitudes?   _____

13. Do I realize how sensitive people really are?   _____

14. Do I permit others to be imperfect?   _____

15. Do I take my right to exercise command?   _____

16. Am I using every experience as a lesson?   _____

17. Do I let other people talk things out with me?   _____

18. Do I remember that people want me to like them?   _____

19. Am I avoiding critical attitudes?   _____

20. Am I working to overcome any shyness I may have?   _____

21. Do I make it easy for another come my way?   _____

22. Do I avoid impulsive judgments of people?   _____

23. Am I shedding false pride daily?   _____

24. Do I laugh enough?   _____

25. Am I discarding unworkable ideas for winning others?   _____

26. Am I filling the other person's need for kindness?   _____

27. Do I clearly plan for avoiding unnecessary troubles?   _____

28. Am I flexible in handling people?   _____

29. Am I taking my responsibility for my own progress?   _____

30. Do I really realize how many problems are avoidable?   _____

Let's look at point 15 as a good example of how you can avoid problems with people. It reads, "Do I take my right to exercise command?"

A man whom we will call Carl was one of those individuals who was continually getting into one unhappy mess after another. He made the mistake of pointing to other people as the cause of his grief. What was the real reason for his failure? Largely, a lack of self-confidence. He was really afraid of people, and therefore powerless with them and therefore in grief of one sort or another. He did not realize that he had a perfect right to command other people.

Carl's confusion expressed itself one day when he told me somewhat indignantly, "I don't think it's right to go around trying to persuade other people. Let them make their own decisions. Live and let live."

"In that case," I told him, "never again listen to a persuasive sermon or political speech. Don't let philosophers such as Emerson and Thoreau talk you into being a better person. Never try to persuade a woman to marry you or a boss to give you a raise. If persuasion is wrong, you have been wrong all your life; you've been trying to win people to your way of thinking since you were one day old. Besides, the real reason you talk so self-righteously is because you are afraid that someone else will try to talk you into doing something you don't want to do. You are speaking from fear and weakness, not from wisdom. Now that we have that out of the way, let's see if we can restore you to the command which you want but don't know how to get."

Carl said he would like that.

A Simple System for Understanding People

Most of us have expressed thoughts like these at one time or another:

"People are funny"

"It takes all kinds."

"Women? I can't figure them out."

"Why do men act like that?"

"I don't understand them at all."

Is it really possible for you to understand people and to use that understanding as an influential tool? Here is what one authority has to say in his book *The Art of Human Relations:*

> One of the chief contributions which psychology, psychiatry, and the study of personality have made to human understanding is the discovery that human behavior *can* be understood, explained, analyzed, and even predicted.[10]

You can clear your path toward commanding power by understanding people better. Not only that but the more we understand a person the more we can like him—and the more he can like us. Haven't you noticed how your insight into another person tends to dislodge your criticism of him when he acts imperfectly? Understanding is the power that enables a parent to love a troublesome child and the virtue that maintains the affection of one spouse for another when domestic difficulties arise.

How do we gain genuine insight into people? That is the vital question we want to answer. Your ability to influence your way in the world depends upon a right answer.

To illustrate, if you drop and lose a small object on the floor, the best way to find it is to set your cheek against the rug and scan its surface. Because the lost object rises above the level of the floor it can be seen quite clearly. Similarly, we can find people to our liking by seeing them from a fresh viewpoint. Here is that new viewpoint that supplies you with powerful insight:

Never pass moral judgment on another. Do not label him as being "cruel" or "immoral" or "conceited." Such labels prevent you from seeing

---

10 Reprinted from *The Art of Human Relations,* copyright 1953, by Henry Clay Lindgren, Thomas Nelson & Sons, Publishers.

the man himself as he really is. It is so easy to attach a label on someone and let it go at that, but this is not the way to understand him. If we are to become astute persuaders we must look beyond the outer effects (such as when someone acts cruelly or with conceit) and find out why a man acts as he does.

Take an extremely cruel and hostile person. All cruelty is based on fear. A man is cruel because he is afraid of something —perhaps he fears a loss of prestige or maybe he is worried lest he fail to succeed in life or maybe he believes that people don't like him. Now then, if you evaluate him as being a "cruel" man you are judging him, and you will have difficulty in persuading him. But if you see him as a *frightened* person, this is quite another thing, for this is not your moral judgment but rather your observation of an actual fact about the man. Notice how much easier you find it to handle a person whom you know to be frightened than a man whom you label as "cruel."

The thing we must do is to replace our moral condemnations with psychological observations—and this is something we must work at constantly. Supposing in your business you run into a customer who is almost persuaded but not quite sold on buying your goods or services. If your mind starts condemning him as being "stubborn," you are going to arouse a certain amount of your own antagonism to him—and if your customer notices it you may lose his good will and possibly the sale.

But let's see what happens when you look beyond his outer show of "stubbornness" to search out the basic motive for his hesitation. You may find perhaps a *doubt* that he can afford your product or maybe a *confusion* as to whether it will serve him as he wishes. By applying the non-judgmental terms of *doubt* and *confusion* you have cleared your own thinking tremendously, for *you have detached your own emotions from the situation* and can hence persuade your man with maximum mental power. Your simple switch in identification places you in charge of both yourself and your customer.

When your car breaks down you do not identify it as being "bad" or "stupid" or "obstinate." If you were to do so you would not know what to do to fix it. Rather, you try to understand what is behind the breakdown. Then, as you adjust the carburetor or clear the block from the gas line you regain power over your car. People are not machines, but this does illustrate the kind of non-judgmental attitude that makes you **a** wise and influential person.

"Judge not that ye be not judged" is not only a religious precept but a 100 percent effective law of life that serves you up with success in your business programs and in your personal affairs.

Here are three more examples for making the big switch:

When another acts unkindly, do not judge him, but rather see him as someone needing to release his painful psychological pressures.

If the other man acts selfishly, do not identify him as being selfish, instead, know that he is too frightened and insecure to be generous.

When someone shows off, do not condemn him, but intelligently see him as a person who needs your attention and approval.

Constantly ask yourself, "Am I judging this person or am I understanding him?" If you want the magic power to master and command people, you will want to understand him.

Be Resourceful and You Won't Be Discouraged

Please turn back to chapter 1 and review the six exciting reasons (page 19) why you should develop your powers of command. There is good reason for doing this. It will spark a fresh flow of enthusiasm; it renews your eagerness to conquer. It makes you want to win, and "Nothing makes men sharper than want." (Joseph Addison) Additionally, "Want awakens the intellect. The keener the want the lustier the growth." (Wendell Phillips)

This self-promoted enthusiasm is but one example of ways in which your resourcefulness can prevent discouragement from slipping into your mind. Discouragement is a condition which we must look into, for it is startling to realize how easily some people throw up their hands in despair after running into a difficulty or two.

Any newly tackled program is bound to include a certain amount of trial and error. You should expect to meet various challenges to your progress, for any other attitude is unrealistic. If you can accept your setbacks as all part of the game, if you do not give in to panic or dismay, you will eventually find yourself on the other side of your problem.

Let me tell you a story about President Lincoln and his resourcefulness.

> In July of 1861, the Northern army suffered a serious defeat in the Battle of Bull Run. The battleground was named after a small stream in northeast Virginia, located only about 30 miles southwest of Washington, D. C. The loss of the battle was doubly shocking to the Union government, for Bull Run was the first major engagement of the Civil War. Confused officers and soldiers straggled in retreat through the capital, passing in the streets some equally shocked government officials and civilians.

> The population of the North was alarmed and distressed at the dreadful news coming from the lips of the beaten soldiers. It was a major disaster, no doubt about that.

> President Lincoln? With characteristic calm he listened to the first reports, then walked to his desk and sat down. Taking pen and paper he paused for a moment to think things through. Then he methodically set down on paper nine clear-cut steps which he believed would relieve the situation. The first of these steps was his recommendation that the United States naval forces immediately set up a blockade of the Southern ports. He urged that the blockade be pushed forward with all possible speed.

Historians agree that the blockade of the Confederate ports was perhaps the greatest single contribution that the Union made toward the winning of the war. And it was Lincoln's resourceful-ness-under-stress that turned the nation from temporary defeat to permanent victory and peace.

Victory and peace in your human relations? That is perfectly possible too. So never give in to gloom whenever you say the wrong thing to someone or when you fail to make a wished-for impression.

Instead, turn the whole thing over to your resourceful mind—which is far more clever than you may think. Take your experiences apart and try to find out what caused them to happen as they did. You can always find some clue for doing much better the next time. If necessary, place your progress before your pride and you will eventually achieve goals of which you can be justly proud. The secret of success in attracting and winning people is really much easier than it appears to be. "The secret of success is constancy to purpose." Those words were spoken by one of the most powerful men who ever influenced world history. His name is Benjamin Disraeli, noted British statesman and favorite of Queen Victoria.

Here is something to remember every minute: People who do not respond to your persuasions are not necessarily disinterested; it may mean that you have not as yet struck the chord that makes them vibrate.

The advertising manager of a Detroit company often uses the following humorous story to illustrate the power of persistence and resourcefulness:

> The waitress of a popular snack shop was determined to persuade a customer to order a dish of ice cream to go with his sandwich. She sensed he was half sold on the idea but needed an extra nudge. She decided to tempt him by suggesting various flavors. The dialogue went like this:
>
> "How about chocolate?"
>
> "No."
>
> "Why not try strawberry?"
>
> "Not interested."
>
> "Like vanilla?"
>
> "No vanilla."
>
> "How about macaroni and cheese?"

"What flavor was that?"

"I said, macaroni and cheese."

"That's just the suggestion I've been waiting to hear!" enthused the customer. "Bring it on!"

How resourceful are you? How many appeals are you willing to try in order to hit the right one? (It may be the last one you expect.) Be sure to keep on playing until you strike the note that produces a harmonizing echo.

Clear Your Way for Rapid Progress

1. Continually look for obstacles which may be blocking your path toward winning people. Remove them and watch your speed.

2. Freely and cheerfully admit that other people are important to you and that you need and want things from them.

3. Remember that the wise way to handle problems is to avoid them in the first place.

4. Use the, check list in this chapter for preventing difficulties from arising in your interpersonal relations.

5. Permit yourself to improve yourself.

6. Constantly look for ways to make it easy for people to come your way. Sometimes all they need is your invitation.

7. Remember that your employment of the principles governing human behavior can prevent problems from arising.

8. Never pass moral judgment on another, for this prevents you from understanding him. Instead, find out why he speaks and behaves as he does. Your knowledge is your power for persuading him.

9. You presently possess all the resources you need for mastering and commanding people, yet you may need to develop them to full capacity.

10. "Those who have finished by making all others think with them have usually been those who began by daring to think for themselves." (Colton)

HOW TO MAKE PEOPLE AGREE WITH WHAT YOU WANT

I want to tell you of a discovery that excited the entire world some years ago. It happened near the village of Cardiff, in the state of New York. This adventure tale will more than entertain you. It will keep you in remembrance of how to make people agree with what you want.

It all started when farmer William C. Newell hired a couple of neighbors to dig a well on his property. They had dug to a depth of only five feet when their shovels hit something hard. Thinking they had struck a boulder they started clearing the earth around the hard mass. As the earth slipped away from the object the two men stepped back, frozen with astonishment. There in front of their wide eyes was the figure of a giant. It was almost 12 feet tall and weighed around 3,000 pounds.

News of the giant's discovery buzzed around the world. Thousands flocked to the site. Several doctors examined the figure and declared it to be a genuine fossil, probably several hundred years old. Their conclusions were backed up by distinguished professors from leading universities. The noted author Oliver

Wendell Holmes looked at the Cardiff Giant and pronounced it a most remarkable find. The farmer whose property had yielded the discovery promptly went into business. Newell erected a tent over the site and happily welcomed the lined-up thousands with a one-dollar peek per passing.

A few experts dared to disagree that the figure was that of a fossilized giant. The President of Cornell University suggested that someone had done a clever bit of sculpturing on a block of stone. He was shouted down. Professor O. C. Marsh of Yale University also refused to accept the Cardiff Giant as genuine. He was ignored.

Tens of thousands of people insisted that *their* opinions were correct: The giant was genuine. Nothing nearly as sensational had hit them during their lives. Here was mystery, delight, and amazement—and they were part of it! No one was going to rob them of their excitement by declaring the giant a fake. They believed in it stubbornly and persistently.

Meanwhile, curious newspaper reporters noticed that a man named George Hull was a partner in exhibiting the discovery. Moreover, he was a cousin of the farmer Newell. Tracing Hull's activities the reporters found that he had shipped a block of gypsum to a Chicago stonecutter, a man named Edward Salle. From Chicago Hull had shipped an immense crate labeled as machinery to Newell's farm.

Faced with the evidence, Hull confessed that the Cardiff Giant was a gigantic hoax. He had ordered the gypsum carved into the shape of a giant, shipped it to Cardiff, kept it buried for a year, then had the laborers dig where sure to find it.

Finally and reluctantly, the believers agreed that they had been fooled. They turned away from the Cardiff Giant with a sad sigh and once more took up their daily duties in their homes and factories and offices.

Why People Behave as They Do—
and How You Can Change Them

Two vital questions spring from this story:

1.   Why do people believe and behave as they do?

2.   How can you persuade them to change their belief and behavior?

Let's first find out why some people cling so stubbornly to their positions and attitudes, even when the facts of the matter clearly contradict their position. By finding out, we will have armed ourselves with ammunition that brings about their willing surrender.

Why did all those people believe in the Cardiff Giant in the first place? Also, why did so many of them persistently defend it even when it had been thoroughly exposed as the fake that it was? The explanation is simple enough: People *wanted* to believe in its genuineness because it added excitement to their otherwise uneventful lives. It was something extraordinary to chat about over the back fence. It gave their imaginations a place to play. It added mystery and a sense of adventure to a somewhat dull existence. As long as their minds were occupied with the Cardiff Giant, they didn't have to think about their daily pains and pressures.

In other words, those people had a deep desire to believe in the giant because to do so gave them a thrilling release from their boredom. They were not interested in what was *true* about the discovery, but only in what was *pleasurable*. Whenever the desire to believe something is accompanied by fun-filled feelings, people eagerly accept whatever is offered to them as truth, regardless of its actual distance from fact and logic. "We believe easily . . . what we desire." (La Fontaine) This is just as much a thinking habit of people today as it was to those who saw the Cardiff Giant. The authors of *Psychology in Business* sum it up,

"People tend to take favorable, or positive, attitudes toward things that give them pleasure and make them feel secure."[11]

What finally changed their minds about the authenticity of the giant? They switched their viewpoint only when it became more profitable *not* to believe than it was *to* believe. For one thing, they didn't want to run the risk of being thought persistently foolish and gullible. Secondly, once the giant was thoroughly exposed, most of the people went along with popular disbelief because to do otherwise would mean to stand alone— and that would make them nervous and insecure. In other words, it finally became more rewarding to disbelieve than to believe.

This last sentence is your chief clue. People believe and behave as they do because of a dominating *desire* or *need* to do so. Their behavior changes only when it is given a superior motive to change.

Another way of saying this is that people take whatever position offers them the greatest personal reward. I once knew a man whose grand passion was a belief in flying saucers from foreign planets. Meet him somewhere and sooner or later he tried to talk you into accepting his theories about strange men from Mars and Venus and other outposts of outer space. One day that man ran across a book extolling the benefits of physical fitness. Having something of a health problem, he became interested in improving his body. Today that man's great passion is health in all its aspects. Meet him today and he tells you why you should eat blackstrap molasses and yoghurt. Today he scarcely cares whether flying saucers exist or not; his new toy is more fun.

Another thing you should know is this: Whenever a person furiously defends his viewpoints or ideas, he doesn't really care much about the ideas themselves. Not really. What he does care about is his personal *identification* with his ideas and beliefs and opinions. This means that what a man is really defending is *himself,* his *ego,* his *self-image* of himself as being this or that sort of worthwhile person. No man defends or roots for a position unless he has first adopted it as his

11 By permission from *Psychology in Business,* by Leslie R. Beach and Elon L. Clark. Copyright 1959. McGraw-Hill Book Company, Inc.

personal position. Once he calls it *my* political party or *my* hometown or *my* family he will defend them against all comers.

Also know this: A highly defensive person can never be persuaded by your calm presentation of the actual facts of a matter because facts played no part in the formation of his original viewpoint—the vital thing for him was that the adopted viewpoint gave him a feeling of security or perhaps a sense of power or maybe a surge of relief from some anxiety. Such a person will not readily submit to the facts of a matter because he feels threatened by them. He thinks like this: "You are not going to cut me adrift from anything that makes me feel secure," or perhaps he declares, "No one is going to make a fool out of me by proving me wrong all these years."

As you can see, no man is going to thank us for attacking those judgments or beliefs which give him such a strong sense of individuality.

What does all this add up to? Just this: Your first objective in winning agreement to your way of thinking is to gently and ever-so-tactfully dislodge a man's attachment to his present position. You do this best, as we saw in Chapter 2, by use of the secret passages. One of the most effective of these is to show him how the adoption of your position will reward him more handsomely than his present standpoint. Prove that your ideas or your plans will supply *greater* security or *additional* prestige or *swifter* financial advancement. Once you do that, his ever-ready desire for self-gain will do *the* rest. You don't have to call twice to bring a hungry man to his dinner.

Offer him *more*. No man is really ever won by any other method. The plain fact is, it takes a superior appeal to a man's self-interest to move him from where he is to where you want him to be.

The Power of Your Promise

Recently after I had concluded a lecture I was approached by a woman with weary lines in her face. Somewhat apologetically she said, "Mr. Howard, in your talk you mentioned something about a barbecue picnic that is coming off next week. Is it open to anyone; I mean, could I come?"

"You are wide-open welcome," I assured her. "I'll see that complete information about time and place is sent you by mail."

She gave an immense sigh of gratitude and relief. "I'll be watching for it. If you only knew how much it means to have something to look forward to. Thank you. It will be enough to keep me going for the next few days."

That weary woman had a deep need for additional strength to see her through her days so filled with lonely duties. The expectation of an exciting tomorrow with its fun and friends was the fulfillment of that need.

This introduces us to the power of your promise. It is something that makes people agreeable to your suggestions and enthusiastic toward your programs.

Whenever you promise something to a man you have used a dynamic force for convincing him that he ought to go along with you. Every man is interested in your pledge that you can make things better or easier or richer for him and his family. It alerts his desire and excites his hope. William Shakespeare proved himself to be as much the masterful persuader as the poet and the dramatist when he wrote, "Promising . . . opens the eyes of expectation ... To promise is most courtly and fashionable. . . ."

The promise is one of the most legitimate and effective means ever devised for winning men's minds. In your hands it becomes an accurate weapon for scoring hits.

Let's take a classic example from history:

Thousands of years ago Moses was in charge of his people as they wandered painfully through the Egyptian wilderness. The aim of this gifted leader was to guide his followers to the land of Canaan. You know the trouble he had. Every step of the way his people grumbled against their lot and rebelled against authority. They were tired. There was too much strain and not enough food. They threatened to give up, to quit, to let the wilderness swallow them up. Every day brought a new crisis in their onward march.

But Moses was a man of solid strength. He also possessed considerable wisdom. He knew a thing or two when it came to handling troubled people.

He promised them something.

He painted a verbal picture of the land that rested on the other side of the wilderness. He told them of its beauty and wealth. Just a few steps more, he assured them, and all shall dwell in a land flowing with milk and honey. That did it. That was all they wanted to hear. They kept going until they reached the Promised Land.

That is how one leader used the power of promise to keep his followers agreeable and cooperative. Let's next see how it works in the commercial world.

Look at an advertisement, for instance, one urging you to buy a particular brand of face soap. When you come right down to it, what is behind the message? It promises you something: A smoother complexion. More popularity. A cleaner feeling. Everyone goes for those things. We like the forecast. So we buy. We have been persuaded by a promise.

You go into a shoe shop. Watch the technique used to sell you. The salesman assures you of greater foot comfort, maybe a savings in price; perhaps he suggests that you will command a few compliments from admiring friends. If the shoes are for your children you may be assured that they are tough enough to withstand all that pounding and scuffing. Because you buy those promises you also buy those shoes.

The reason a promise is so compelling is because a man knows that he cannot personally tell how things are going to turn out before he personally experiences them—he is therefore eager for your assurance that he will end up happily rewarded. He wants you to tell him *beforehand* how great he will feel later as a result of his agreement with you. Your promise is his relief.

Needless to add, your fulfilled promise is going to make you doubly influential with the person who has just had his hopes aroused by you. You can win a man's confidence by offering him a reward for going along with you, but you keep his loyalty by making good on your offer.

"Promises are . . . necessary for the comfort and security of mankind." (Earl of Clarendon)

Thirty Sure Ways to Get Others to Say Yes to You

There is the story of the ardent lover who was trying to persuade his new lady-love to share the evening with him. Their dialogue went like this:

"You are beautiful. Pick you up at six?"

"Never."

"We'll have hours of fun. Six o'clock all right?"

"No."

"You'll meet some exciting people.   How about six?"

"Won't."

"You are one in a million.   Six o'clock about right?"

"Can't."

"We'll have an enchanting evening.   Shall we say six?"

"Maybe."

"I like you more and more. Pick you up at six?"

"Six."

Maybe that is an exaggerated version of the way things might actually go, but it does spotlight some techniques by which you can win an affirmative answer in almost any situation. Notice that it includes several basic principles governing persuasiveness, including *persistence*, the *promise of excitement,* and a *contribution to the other persons self-esteem.*

There are sure ways to get others to say *yes* to you. You will discover them in this section.

Stop and think of just about everything you own and you will see that they came your way by means of your personal request. You asked for it, in one way or another, and got what you asked for. Making requests of other people is a daily necessity for all of us. The baby sets off the well-heard howl to get his bottle. The young man coos sweet-talk in the moonlight and gets his girl to agree to share a honeymoon cottage with him. The baker wafts the delicious aroma of freshly baked bread your way and that is how he asks you to buy.

We ask for things from almost everyone we meet. We want another's attention or cooperation or companionship or maybe his name on the dotted line. If the other person says *yes* we are much happier than if he says *no.*

It is fairly obvious that our requests of other people are pretty important to our daily welfare.

But the really important thing is to get the right answer to a request. And the right answer is, of course, *yes.*

Getting another to give you the affirmative nod is easier than you think. That is the viewpoint you should adopt first of all. As someone once put it, "Whenever you ask for something from someone there can be only two definite answers—he can say *yes* or he can say *no.* So even before you begin you have a fifty-fifty chance of getting what you want. A bit of practice on your part and you'll soon be commanding the other fifty percent."

Think of the particular person (or group of people) whom you wish to win over to your side. Keep him in mind as you go through the following punchy pointers. Check off those suggestions which you think are especially valuable in winning your man to your way. Now, throw them into service the very next time you meet the one whom you wish to win.

1. Find and keep his attention.

2. Let him know you appreciate his cooperation.

3. Remove any serious objections he may have.

4. Make your plan sound exciting and adventurous.

5. Frankly ask for his help in promoting your plan.

6. Make yourself as attractive as your program.

7. Offer the richest possible reward for going your way.

8. Show him how others have benefited from your plan.

9. Keep your appeal simple and easy to understand.

10. Let him know that you will back up his cooperation.

11. Promise definite benefits for the future.

12. Present a personal appearance of confidence.

13. Repeatedly show him his need for your program.

14. Avoid all appearance of apology for your plan.

15. Keep him in the center of your appeal.

16. Be genuinely interested in him.

17. Permit him to be relaxed with you.

18. Act as if you expect an answer of yes.

19. Use every refusal as an opportunity to try again.

20. Present a friendly appearance.

21. Promise immediate benefits from your program.

22. Appeal to his need for something new.

23. Make it clear that you are not taking but giving.

24. Permit him to express freely his opinions.

25. Avoid pressuring him.

26. Keep thinking from his viewpoint.

27. Be natural.

28. Contribute to his self-esteem.

29. Prove why it is best to agree with you.

30. Let him know you enjoy his company.

I was once acquainted with a top-ranked businessman whose hobby took him to the spacious back yard of his suburban home. In a special section of that backyard there was a vegetable garden. There was only one kind of vegetable in that garden—tomatoes—but what tomatoes! There were without the slightest doubt the largest, prettiest, and tastiest tomatoes in the state. The ladies of the neighborhood eagerly waited for the day when he picked and passed around his superb tomatoes. His garden and its fabulous harvest made the local newspapers more than once.

Quite naturally he was asked how he had persuaded nature to yield to him so richly. He replied, "The secret of all success is to set up a high goal and then concentrate everything you have on it. I wanted to have the biggest and best tomatoes that nature could yield, so I concentrated on that one thing and that one thing only. I studied tomatoes constantly. I experimented with various types of seeds. I found out what tomatoes need for top nutrition and gave it to them. I cultivated tomatoes with a single-minded purpose. The fact is, I cannot fail. Anyone else could get the same miraculous results if he would set his mind on that single purpose. Nature yields to the man who constantly searches out her secrets."

This story illustrates what concentration can do in the natural world, but the same principle works just as miraculously for the man who applies it in the world of people. Any man who consistently follows the rules set down in this chapter cannot fail to possess the magic power to master and command people.

What you want is for others to say *yes* to you.

So concentrate on ways to get what you want.

It will be the beginning of fresh power for you and the ending of scarcity.

How to Get Around the Other Man's Objections

There is one golden rule that can place you in command of the person who raises an objection to the plan you are trying to put across. Learn it well and you will have taken a long stride toward persuading him to go along with you.

That rule is: *Never make a big thing of a man's unreasonable objection.* Regardless of how forcefully he may state it, do not add to his force by making a strong objection to his objection.

There are times of course when a man raises an entirely reasonable objection which you will want to answer in one way or another. This you can easily do, for a reasonable man is always open to a reasonable answer. For instance, a man once questioned my judgment in advising him to use his spare cash to clear off the mortgage on his home. He wanted to use the money for investment purposes. When I showed him the actual figures on how much money he would save on interest payments he readily agreed that my suggestion was a good one.

However, just now we are not talking about the reasonable type of objection; we want to discover the best way to handle the confused or the highly emotional type of individual. Let's face it, we sometimes run into difficult people along the way, but we need not be bothered by them once we get their number.

To repeat the rule, never make a big thing out of a man's illogical objections. You would not add more wood to a blazing forest fire, and neither should you add fuel to the objection by feeding it with your attention. When you argue over it or even give it your attention by talking about it you make it seem important to the other man. Your very emphasis makes him think his position is far more valid than it actually may be. Inside himself he thinks, "Say, I must have a solid objection here, otherwise, why would he be so impressed as to attack it?" This prods him into doubling the force of his resistance, which is the very last thing you want him to do.

Make this experiment the next time you run into an objection from someone whom you are trying to persuade. Whenever he takes exception to your plan, simply ignore whatever he says, just as if he didn't say it at all. Blithely go on to a positive idea, one that appeals to him. You will find that in a surprising number of cases he won't mention it again. Why does he drop it? Because your refusal to give it importance makes it seem unimportant to him also. Your very silence dissolves his objection in a way that a direct attempt could never accomplish.

One advertising man has a remarkably high score when it comes to making people agree with what he wants. No doubt there are a number of reasons for his steady successes, but one of them is different enough to be studied. To state it as simply as possible, he has the habit of acting as if he never hears himself getting turned down. That interesting character trait contributes to his power to win his way.

> He explains it like this: "I explain my services and the man tells me *no.* Somehow I just don't hear him. I casually go on with my sales presentation. He repeats that he's sorry, but he's just not interested. I act as if he said something about the weather and bring up another point in favor of his taking on my services. He tells me that he doesn't think he can afford it just now and I show him the latest plan we have for putting his business in the

spotlight. Before long that man is so bewildered by my density that he signs the order just to clear his own head."

The advertising man explains in conclusion, "If you don't hear your customer tell you *no,* you just can't possibly be discouraged—so just don't hear it. Don't give the word *no* any meaning. It's interesting how many times your man will forget what he's talking about and start buying what *you're* talking about."

You may some day find yourself in a position where you will have to answer an unreasonable objection publicly. Every leader among men sometimes finds himself confronted with a difficult or confused person who makes up part of any audience. Such a man likes to draw attention to himself by asking pointless questions or by trying to trick the man in charge of the meeting. The first thing to realize, of course, is that you are dealing with a person of low self-esteem. He sometimes uses public occasions to bolster his faltering ego. How do you handle such a person? Obviously he cannot be completely ignored. His statement—no matter how unreasonable—must be met and answered in the right way. So how do you remove his public objections.

Actually, he can be quite easily handled. What you must do is to ignore the *seriousness* of his statement or question. Don't take him as if he really means it, for he really has no desire to get a responsible reply—he just wants others to look his way.

In my own talks and lectures I sometimes run into such a situation. I find that the humorous reply handles things nicely:

At one time I had been invited to address a businessmen's luncheon club in a California city. The program chairman warned me beforehand that a certain member of the club had the habit of heckling the speaker. He asked me to please understand and not be offended. I assured him I understood perfectly. Sure enough, during the question-and-answer period the man got to his feet, made some sort of a vague objection, then told me, "I think you have a superiority complex."

Putting on a facial expression of intense conviction, I replied, "No, I don't have a complex—I really *am* superior."

That drew a laugh from the audience, of course, but the chief value in the reply was that it answered that objection by treating it according to its own nature, that is, non-seriously.

Try this system for yourself. See how much better you can remove a man's unreasonable objections by refusing to be impressed by them.

Summary of Steps for Winning Your Way

1. Remember that people tend to believe what they want and need to believe. To persuade them, build up their need for whatever you have to offer.

2. To change another's viewpoint, show him how your way will reward him more than his present way. Appeal to his desire for a change for the better.

3. Persuade by the power of your promise. Present people with an exciting picture of what they can expect to gain.

4. Take the attitude that it is easier to influence people than you may think. It really is, once you know what to do.

5. Back up your product or program with a self-confident personality.

6. Keep your appeal simple and to the point.

7. Establish an atmosphere of friendliness and relaxation.

8. Prove to the other person that you are here to give him something, not merely to take.

9. Concentrate wholeheartedly on the principles of persuasion.

10. Never strongly object to the other person's unreasonable objection. Quietly step aside and let it pass harmlessly by.

YOU CAN BE QUICKLY LIKED AND APPRECIATED

A somewhat confused man once asked me, "Why should I care whether or not anyone likes me? I have enough money to live comfortably; I manage to keep myself busy; why should I bother whether anyone likes me?"

"Because," I told him, happiness is always better than misery. Of course you may have your money and your activities, but are you happy? Anyone can keep *busy*, but are you *happy?*"

He said he wasn't sure.

Of course that man cared—and cared desperately—whether or not people liked him. Underneath his thin coating of indifference lurked that persistent human yearning to be valued and appreciated by others. His problem was in his confusion as to how to achieve one of life's simplest but greatest of prizes-warm and gratifying relations with people.

Being wanted and needed by other people is vital to personal health and happiness. Still, it is only one side of the golden coin. What is the other part? What is just as necessary as having someone to like us? It is *having someone to like*. As Douglas Jerrold writes, "It is the beautiful necessity of our nature to love something." Every river needs an outlet for its flow; every individual needs someone upon whom he can release affections and kindnesses and services. Every man or woman who silently requests of another, "Please like me," also asks with equal yearning, "Please—will you let me like you?"

> Thomas Edison was once asked by a laboratory assistant why certain basic principles should be applied when working with electricity. "You should follow the rules," the great inventor replied, "because they work."

There has never been a better reason for applying any set of rules than that they do what they are supposed to do. So let's adventure into those fundamental principles governing human relations which can make any person quickly liked and appreciated—and which also supply him with someone to whom he can say, "I like you."

It is the likeable people who are the most persuasive.

Likeability List

We sometimes get so involved with complicated plans for building an attractive personality that we forget the use of those every-day pleasantries which appeal automatically to everyone. It is really the simplest task in the world to win the friendship and approval of those whom we want to attract. All you really have to do to be liked is to be likeable.

Use the following list of attractive traits of personality. Read each of these powers of persuasion (that is what they really are) and rate yourself from 1 to 5. If you feel that you possess the likeable trait to a maximum degree, score yourself with a 5. To lesser degrees, rate yourself 1, 2, 3, 4.

Give special attention to those having the lowest ratings, then decide that you will raise them to maximum power. Connect your endeavors with some of the self-advancing techniques supplied throughout this book.

We are liked best when we are:

	1	2	3	4	5
1. Dependable					
2. Natural					
3. Undemanding					
4. Calm					
5. Helpful					
6. Courageous					
7. Modest					
8. Respectful					
9. Composed					
10. Attentive					
11. Diplomatic					
12. Responsible					
13. Sincere					
14. Decisive					
15. Loyal					
16. Sociable					
17. Encouraging					
18. Discreet					
19. Enthusiastic					
20. Optimistic					
21. Prompt					
22. Reliable					
23. Understanding					
24. Fair-minded					
25. Compassionate					

	1	2	3	4	5
26. Enterprising					
27. Consistent					
28. Lively					
29. Approving					
30. Earnest					
31. Considerate					
32. Simple-mannered					
33. Cheerful					
34. Relaxed					
35. Generous					
36. Patient					
37. Cooperative					
38. Peaceful					
39. Courteous					
40. Energetic					
41. Polite					
42. Adventurous					
43. Gentle					
44. Entertaining					
45. Approachable					
46. Uncomplicated					
47. Responsive					
48. Cordial					
49. Reasonable					
50. Self-commanding					

Be Simple and Spontaneous

One of the aims of this book is to show you how to present a personality that is naturally attractive, one that is unencumbered by mental confusions and emotional barriers. When you come right down to it, the people who are liked best are those who walk among others with a free and simple and spontaneous and easy-going self. But this does not at all mean that simple people lack vigor and sparkle; on the contrary, they possess much more of these natural attractions than complicated individuals. The complex personality chokes off his natural forces of spontaneity and freshness. It is a man's original and natural state to possess the traits previously listed, such as calmness of spirit and an adventurous attitude toward life.

To repeat, it is the simple things, the elementary things, the direct and spontaneous things that have the most influence on us. It is curious that we as human beings forget this. We forget and neglect it because we ourselves have become complex and indirect. In this state we have little capacity to see things simply and directly.

All this is leading up to a very practical point, which is this: As we regain our simplicity of personality, we become extremely aware of ways and means to attract and influence others. Our personal simplicity enables us to work with others in a straightforward and immensely effective manner.

I want to show you what I mean:

While on my way to a speaking engagement I was driving through a small town when I decided to stop for lunch. Although the town itself was of limited size, it had a busy main street, for it was the passageway between two large cities. I took a booth in a modest-sized cafe and began making some notes for a new manuscript I was working on. The man who took my order turned out to be the owner. He made some sort of a friendly remark about my notes, after which I told him that I wrote books on the subject of practical psychology.

"Practical psychology," he reflected. "That's just what I need. Maybe you can help me. I'm always looking for ways to attract more customers. We get lots of tourists and travelers through here. I'd like to induce more of them to stop in here for lunch. How can I do it? If I'm not asking too much, could you give me just one good idea for bringing them in?"

I asked him to come outside with me. As we stood on the sidewalk facing his cafe, I requested, "Take a look at your sign."

He glanced up at his sign which read *Dans Cafe*. "Yes," he nodded, "what about it?"

"How big is it?"

"About two feet in height."

"Make it four."

He frowned, "Four feet tall? That's a big sign for such a small cafe."

"No, I don't mean four feet. I mean four yards."

"Four yards in height?"

"Four yards. In bright red letters. Are you interested in conforming to the usual pattern or are you interested in catching more customers?"

He whistled. "You're right. Why didn't I think of that before?"

"Because your mind is caught in traditional thinking patterns. Just because the man down the street has a two-foot sign is no reason why you should follow him. In fact, it's the best reason for *not*. You want to win more customers? Good.

Do it the simple way. Attract their attention with a sign that attracts attention. You're not being brash. You're being independent. And businesslike."

"Your lunch," he told me excitedly, "is on the house."

Summary: Look for the obvious and the simple and the direct thing to do. That is what attracts people who can do things for you.

Be Casual With People

To be casual with people simply means that we accept them as they are. It means that we don't insist that they behave according to our ideas of right behavior. It also means that we don't try to force them to occupy the place we want them to occupy for our own comfort or convenience.

You are dealing in a mature fashion with other people when you handle them causally, rather than forcefully.

In Japan's pearl industries they use wide boards perforated with holes of various sizes. The purpose of these boards is to permit the pearls to find their own places in the world of jewelry. As the gems roll down the incline they fall automatically into the proper opening, in other words, they drop through the board into the box where they naturally belong. Damage would be done to both the pearl and the industry if workers insisted on forcing the pearls into this or that opening. The wise worker casually and simply permits each gem to behave as it chooses. He then uses it according to its own choice of behavior.

Likewise, we should never try to force anyone into a position which we think they should occupy, rather, we must let them be themselves. When you come to think of it, it is the only fair way. After all, we want them to let *us* be ourselves!

One way to achieve this casual sort of acceptance is to give people credit for the roles they *do* play; appreciate them for what they *are*, and don't be distressed over what you think they *should* be.

Give casual credit.

It has been said that you could send a telegram with the single word "Congratulations" on it to 10 different people and all of them could think of a valid reason for it. Most people feel that the credit they get lags sadly behind the credit they deserve. This means that the person who appreciates the efforts of another is certain to be appreciated in return.

It is easy enough to praise another whenever he achieves something unusual, but the kindest credit of all is that given to another for his little daily tasks, like turning out accurate office reports day after day, or like the cooking and cleaning carried on by the faithful little lady around the home.

People don't really ask too much from life. When you come right down to it, most of us are blissfully content with the simple life once our needs for self-esteem and self-worth have been fulfilled.

"Good things should be praised." (Shakespeare) Give a man credit for his daily tasks and you turn him into a happy and appreciative individual. You also make him your friend.

"I Like You the Way You Are"

If there are seven beautiful words in this world, you have just read them. There is absolutely nothing like them for making people want to be with you and to be for you.

People get so weary of other people who are always trying to change them. People get plain sick and tired of being criticized, accused, glared at, contradicted, bawled out, blamed, imposed upon, restricted, ridiculed, turned down, judged, laughed at, doubted, cold-shouldered, snapped at, prohibited, and penalized.

If any of these have ever happened to you, you get the point.

A woman once told me, "Whenever I meet someone, I always hope he likes *me*, not the me he wants me to be."

When you offer others simple acceptance of themselves with all their habits and moods and opinions you have given them something for which they have been desperately searching all their lives. When your attitude and manner tell someone, "Please be yourself, whatever that self may be," you have set yourself apart in his eyes as a person with extraordinary kind ness and understanding.

An executive in the electrical equipment industry passes on this word to his department supervisors:

> Always assure your new employees from the very start that we expect them to have human faults. Let them know that as far as the company is concerned there is no such thing as an awkward beginner; there is only an employee who is getting on to the hang of things. This relieves a good deal of the tension that usually goes along with the tackling of a new skill. Our employees will learn much faster and will be far happier and more efficient.

That company has proved over the years that it's even good business to like and accept people the way they are.

Besides all this, the more you take the other person as he is, the more you will understand him. And the more you grasp the ways he works, the more influence you are going to exert. People themselves will tell you how to win them over. But you have to listen.

How To Be Enchanting

I recall one time as a boy I had gone to the movie theater to see the latest mystery film. The plot concerned a gang of international jewel thieves who were plotting to steal the crown jewels from the Tower of London. A chum of mine, a fun-loving boy named Donny, sat down next to me and began chomping on a candy bar.

"Good picture," he gulped between bites.

"Quiet," I scowled. "I want to watch."

A moment later he asked, "Know who's going to do it?"

"Do what?"

He pointed his candy bar at the screen.   "Do the big robbery."

"Go away."

"You'll never guess," he gulped. "Don't want to," I growled. "Vanish." He threatened with a grin, "I think I'll tell you." I threatened with a frown, "You do and you'll be sorry." Donny jabbed a finger at the moving figures, "See that man with the mustache?"

I turned on him with a glare, "Donny, if you . . ." "Well," Donny laughed, "he isn't the one." As I sat back in relief, Donny leaped up, shook a sticky finger at the screen, yelled, "The woman with the earrings! She did it! Eeeeee!" With the fiendish yelp Donny dodged out of reach of my clutching hands. It was good for his health that he did, for he had ruined the mystery. Now that I knew who was going to pull off the big operation, my level of interest dropped at least 50 percent.

The point is this: Don't give yourself away completely. While everyone likes the forthright and clear-cut individual, remember also that "There is profound charm in mystery." (Chat-field) You shouldn't tell everyone everything about yourself; keep them guessing a bit. You are entitled to your private life and others are entitled to be somewhat curious about it. Their curiosity will keep them wanting to associate more in order to learn more. Hand a clipped newspaper to someone and he will hound you for the clipped-out item.

Women have mastered this secret better than men, for they seem to sense that "It is the dim haze of mystery that adds enchantment to pursuit." (Rivarol)

Be Someone Special

The humorous story goes about the weary hostess who was told by a guest, "I notice that your next door neighbor doesn't seem to have many friends,"

Replied the hostess with a sigh, "Yes; I wonder how she manages."

Most people are not interested in having an unlimited number of friends and acquaintances. Not really. Even when a man firmly declares his interest in being surrounded constantly by lots of people he may not realize how he is kidding himself. Even while mixing gaily with the crowd he secretly hopes to find one person—just the right person—who will like him and accept him and understand him and who will tell him that he is pretty much okay after all. When and if he finds that one special friend, his driving need for so many others slackens off.

One way to be a special person is to be a *reassuring* friend. That automatically makes you stand out in any crowd. It is a fact that for every 10 people who need reassurance of their personal worth there is usually only one person around who is capable of saying and doing the things that fill that need. That one person is easily someone special.

"Assurance is more than life. It is health, strength, power, vigor, activity, energy." (J. C. Ryle) Think of how much a man will like you when you give him all that!

A man whom we'll call Tom walked in with drooping shoulders and sad eyes. "Mr. Howard," he began, "I've tried to be a success in life. Really I've tried. Hard. But I no longer know which way to turn. I'm confident only in doing today what I did yesterday. And yesterday was a flop. I don't mean to burden you with my problems, but sometimes I get so discouraged over making a success of my life . . ." His voice trailed off.

"I don't think you understand," I told him.

"Understand what?"

"That you *are* a success. A success I appreciate."

"What do you mean?"

"You're a success with me. Completely."

Tom smiled. "I guess you're just trying to make me feel good."

"That wasn't my primary purpose. I have my own definition of a successful man. As far as I'm concerned, his only qualification is to be a nice kind of person. A friendly man or a pleasant woman is an instant and overwhelming success with me. That's why you are a genuine success."

"Nice," he smiled with assurance, "to hear it phrased like that."

Build your own self-assurance through the techniques of this book (Chapter 10 especially) and you will become a very special person to others. "Please be stronger than I," is the hope and plea of practically everyone who ever contacts anyone. If you will go right ahead and satisfy that hope you will have progressive popularity.

Decide to Expand Yourself Through People

You should insist to yourself that you are going to expand your power to persuade and command people. Regardless of what you want—whether it is appreciation or financial increase or social popularity—you can advance beyond your present position spectacularly. There is no such thing as limitation, there is only an apparent border rimming your circle of success. You can break through this seeming enclosure by starting right where you are and by employing *new* people and *more* people.

You must guard against too much self-satisfaction in your present programs with others. Present successes tend to blunt your effort toward greater ones to be found in the future. Keep challenging yourself. Start every morning with a fresh attack. New challenges breed toughness, alertness, and best of all they breed new victories in your financial or social world or wherever else you want them.

Some years ago there was an enthusiastic merchant named Richard who lived in Redwood Falls, Minnesota. He made small but steady profits by buying coal and lumber from the local Indians and selling them to all customers he could find. Richard was pleased with his success, but not overly content with it. Being the enthusiastic businessman that he was, he wanted fast growth. Richard started looking around for opportunities to expand himself by selling more goods to more people. One day the jeweler in Redwood Falls refused to accept a shipment of watches sent to him by the manufacturer. Sensing an opportunity, Richard promptly hurried over. He received permission to sell the watches, then sat down to write some enthusiastic letters describing the timely bargains. People that he had never even seen started sending him money by return mail. When the entire lot was sold, Richard happily saw that his expansion could be pushed by the simple process of contacting people beyond his present commercial world. He immediately bought more watches and quickly sold them at a nice profit by advertising in the St. Paul newspapers. Business boomed. Richard moved to Chicago to set himself up in the mail order business. Today, that business is big business, for that young man's full name was Richard W. Sears, the founder of Sears, Roebuck and Company.

Likewise, you can expand your success. People whom you have not yet met are quite willing to be persuaded by you. Do your part in contacting them with an attractive offer and they will do the rest.

There is really no limit to your possibilities of success with people. The obstacles are mainly mental. Clear your mind and you clear your way.

Vital Ideas For Your Review

1. It is vital to health and happiness to have people in our lives who like our ways and who appreciate our company.

2. It is equally vital that our lives include people whom we can enjoy.

3. Use the Likeability List to build your powers of persuasion.

4. Always do the simple, obvious thing to win others. Being fair-minded and considerate are examples of obviously effective methods.

5. Give people casual credit. Tell them they are doing just fine. They need to hear it. They like the person who tells them so.

6. It is not our duty in life to force others to change their ways. It is our pleasure to like them. If they need to change, to like them is the best way to change them.

7. Keep your private affairs to yourself.

8. Be someone special to someone. You are a special per son when you are approachable and undemanding and dependable and reasonable.

9. Decide to expand your fortunes through contacts with new people.

10. Remember that there is no limit to your likeability. Everyone, without exception, possesses vast quantities of attractive traits of personality which can be released more and more.

6
Chapter

HOW TO WIN OVER THE
OPPOSITE SEX

Recently at a social affair, seven or eight of us were off to one side of the main party discussing life in general. The topic of conversation eventually drifted around to male-female relationships. When one of the women discovered that I wrote books on the topic of human relations, she addressed herself to me somewhat cynically:

"You know, now that I think about it, I don't think I like men very much."

"Why not?" I asked.

She said, "Want to know something? Whenever a man takes me out for the evening I know just what he has on his mind."

"Want to know something?" I replied. "Every woman since Eve has known just what a man has on his mind. Furthermore, no emotionally healthy woman would have it any other way. It does so much for her feminine self-esteem. The very fact that you bring it up proves that. It also proves that you have the very same thing on your mind. Now that we've clarified your thinking, let's see if we can help with your problem."

Clear and realistic thinking by one sex toward the other is essential if their mutual persuasions are to return a mutual enrichmerit. For instance, there is no place for bitterness born of past experiences, for if it is carried over into a present relationship it will embitter that new one also. That, unfortunately, is often what happens, leaving both parties sorrowfully wondering what happened to their fun together.

Half the world is made up of the sex opposite your own, which is a pretty wonderful arrangement any way you look at it. That is why your program of people-persuasion should include an understanding of the opposite sex. A man limits his possibilities until he discovers the secrets of appealing to women. A woman misses the mark far too often unless she knows how to get around the men in her life.

The principles laid down in other chapters of this book are generally applicable to both men and women. For instance, all of us wish to advance ourselves economically; everyone has a need for fresh experiences; both men and women need to be liked and approved. These are general principles which can be used to win over either sex.

However, this chapter adventures into the specific relationship between a man and a woman. It should prove to be both an interesting and helpful investigation. A major portion of our happiness in life depends upon the successful handling of him or her.

A man must learn to persuade a woman by appealing to her feminine qualities.

A woman should master the art of influencing a man by employing man-winning methods.

This leads us to the stimulating question:

What Do You Think of the Opposite Sex?

It has been said that there is only one way to handle a woman, but the trouble is, nobody knows what it is.

We can go beyond that humorous idea to discover that effective methods for handling men and women really do exist.

A good deal of the success you will have in winning over the opposite sex will be determined by the attitudes you hold toward men and women. This means the *real* attitudes, the ones you hold in secret within yourself. As a matter of fact, attitudes are the single greatest areas where everyone can brighten his personality and thus sharpen his persuasiveness. Why are viewpoints so vital a part of male-female relations? Because our attitudes determine our behavior and also our speech and even our facial expressions. If our behavior is dull or negative, we lose; but if our actions are inspiring and attractive, we win. The outer self is always determined by the inner self. And the inner self consists largely of attitudes of one kind or another.

The winning attitude is the one we discussed in Chapter 3, that is, dealing with another person without labeling him as being "good" or "bad" or anything else. We are able to understand another only as we cease to judge or moralize or criticize him.

When we moralize against another we miss the point; we see him as *we* are, not as *he* is. Moreover, we must get our adopted ideas of what is "right" and "wrong" out of the way if we are to achieve our maximum powers of persuasion.

Couples who disagree with each other sometimes ask me to tell them which one is "right." I ask them to think of themselves as having *different* viewpoints, rather than "right" or "wrong" ones. This is non-judgmental (and kindly) thinking at its best.

Let's look into an example of how an attitude of understanding can establish and maintain smooth relations.

Supposing you have a loved one or perhaps a close friend who makes life difficult for you. Perhaps this person is somewhat unstable, alternating between fight and flight. Maybe he or she tends to be extremely sensitive, gets his feelings hurt easily. Maybe he has a habit of withdrawing in wounded pride after a disagreement. Such a person is bound to resist your efforts at kindly persuasion, he tends to be fixed and unyielding. No matter how patient you may be, you just can't get through to him.

What makes him like this? Why, you wonder, would anyone resist someone who wants to be nice to him? Why would anyone refuse to be loved?

Dr. Sidney M. Jourard sheds the light of understanding by pointing out:

> It may seem surprising to the reader that some individuals find it hard, if not impossible, to accept love which is freely given by others; yet such is the case . . . When someone loves them, they become suspicious of the lover—the lover may be just pretending to love in order to disarm him and make him vulnerable. Or the lover may be trying to get the individual to do something. The person who cannot accept love may hold the false assumption that to accept love implies that one needs love, and to need love means one is weak.[12]

Because such a person has been hurt in past experiences with the opposite sex he tends to resist newly-offered love for fear of getting hurt again. Hostile people and withdrawn people are really hurt people. They desperately need someone who understands and treats them as such.

If you will understand just this much about a loved one, you will possess an attitude that can influence your relationship toward harmony and pleasure.

Your Persuasive Words

Have you ever thought of your daily words as being *attitudes?* That is exactly what they are. The words we speak to others are extensions of the viewpoints and convictions we harbor within.

In Chapter 14 we will go into detail concerning the power of your words for influencing another, but now let's examine some examples of love-inspiring words. Nothing is more evident than that your

---

12 Sidney M. Jourard, *Personal Adjustment* (New York: The Macmillan Company, 1958). Reprinted by permission of the publisher.

daily words are unlimited forces for winning your way. Sometimes a carelessly spoken word can depress a friendly relationship, but another word gently whispered can restore peace to that relation. "Words are mighty; words are living." (Proctor) Try thinking of the phrases listed below as being *spoken* words rather than merely printed ones. When spoken in sincerity by a man to a woman, or vice versa, they become warmly penetrating forces. Find the correct time and circumstance and employ these persuasive words, gentle words, loving words, and most welcome words:

"I love you."

"You're one in a million."

"I like you."

"You delight me"

"I miss you."

"I'll wait for you"

"I need you."

"Tell me about yourself."

"You're exciting."

"I understand."

"You're nice."

"I want you."

"I've been thinking of you."

"I'll phone you."

"It's good just being with you."

You are a much kinder person than you may think you are. This is not flattery; this is a fact. Within every person are vast stores of natural affection. They may be hampered by confused attitudes or hidden by hurtful experiences of the past, but they are there and always will be there, ready for release upon call.

Remember that you win over the opposite sex when you:

1.   Hold affirmative and kindly attitudes.

2.   Express them freely and confidently.

Once a man or a woman discovers the real self, the genuinely kindly and loving self, a wonderful transformation takes place in their acts and attitudes toward the opposite sex. I am thinking of a couple who had the usual difficulties understanding each other, but who had at least the beginnings of mature and considerate attitudes toward each other.

One day when they dropped in for an informal chat, I asked them how things were going.

The woman replied, "Much better. Really."

"You know," the man added, "it's interesting how our outlooks toward each other have changed. What a difference."

"In what way?" I asked.

"Well, we used to get distressed because of the one or two little things that went wrong between us."

"And now?"

"Now we enjoy the hundred and one things that go right. We never really realized that for everything that went wrong between us, there were at least one hundred things that went right. That is what we now concentrate on—and enjoy."

Men: What You Should Know About Women!

No matter how much you may think you know about a woman, there just might be a few things she's kept to herself. That is why you might make some fresh discoveries in the following list. Here is your short course in feminine psychology. Use it to build the masculine charm that attracts feminine delight. You can always believe that:

1. She hopes you need her.

2. She likes you to be decisive in character.

3. She takes things very personally.

4. She is not really as confident as she acts.

5. She wants you to take care of her.

6. She sees through you more than you think.

7. She likes to dramatize things.

8. She can he understood by you.

9. She worries what people think of her.

10. She often resists in order to prove your persistence.

11. She awaits your tenderness.

12. She wants you to be smoothly aggressive.

13. She cannot take excessive criticism.

14. She sees ten times more than she tells.

15. She is more puzzled by life than appears.

16. She is really a pretty timid girl.

17. She can be persuaded by you.

18. She worries that life is passing her by.

19. She is suspicious of you and maybe with good reason.

20. She feels constantly insecure.

21. She wants you to prefer her above all others.

22. She is romantic-minded.

23. She is afraid of getting her feelings hurt.

24. She is often inconsistent in behavior.

25. She likes praise and compliments.

26. She often doubts that you love her.

27. She likes surprises from you.

28. She is often more emotional than logical.

29. She wants you to take the initiative.

30. She needs constant reassurance of your love.

31. She takes life more seriously than she wants.

32. She resists being ordered to do anything.

33. She is quite sensitive to disapproval.

34. She needs to talk things out.

35. She does not understand herself too well.

36. She can be rather subtle at times.

37. She is bothered by making decisions.

38. She tries sincerely to improve herself.

39. She welcomes your affections.

40. She has a lively interest in sex.

Point 12 points out, *She wants you to be smoothly aggressive.* Every man should remember and never, never forget:

A woman is never so disappointed in a man as when she expects him to act boldly toward her and he doesn't. She is usually wanting and hoping that he will be daring toward her, even though half the time she intends beforehand to turn him down. The man who gets places with his lady is the one who is so genuinely bold that he can approach her without the slightest concern whether or not she will turn him down. Quite often that is just the thing that wins her; she surprisingly yields to the nonchalant male who doesn't give a hoot whether she yields or not.

If you were to ask advice from the great lovers of all times, men like Casanova and Don Juan, they would enthusiastically agree: "Above all things that women respond to, nothing attracts and delights and wins them more than a man's sheer audacity."

Every man should remember that he is being both bold and persuasive when he offers verbal bouquets like those listed previously. He should not be afraid to be generously tender with his lady-love. Lots of men are much too hesitant. Writes Dr. Ernest Dichter, "A great many people do not give because they are afraid of seeing themselves as soft-hearted... we are ashamed to say, 'I love you.'"[13] The best way in the world to have someone tenderly speak those nice words to you is to have the freedom and courage to say them yourself first.

In point 30 we find that a woman needs to be constantly reminded and reassured of your devotion toward her. She wants to be shown that it's there. Telling her of your liking for her is one way to do it,

---

13 Ernest Dichter, *The Strategy of Desire* (New York: Doubleday and Company, Inc., 1960).

for as Voltaire pointed out, "The ear is the avenue to the heart." The simple courtesy of paying attention to her problems and also to her enthusiasm is another. Treating her with patience and consideration are always wonder-working expressions of love. In more intimate relations, there are few things as convincing to a woman as those delightful expressions which we call hugs and kisses.

You can also show a woman how much she means to you by making her someone special:

Two soldiers marched off to war. When one of them returned he told his dream-girl, "Dear, I was lonely."

When the other marched home he sought out his sweetheart and whispered tenderly into her ear, "Dear, I was lonely for *you.*"

That, in brief, is the difference between the amateur and the professional lady-persuader.

There is no display quite as wonderful as a display of affection. As we saw in a previous paragraph, some people, men especially, hesitate to openly display such emotions as fondness and tenderness. They mistakenly believe that such expressions indicate weakness. The exact opposite is true. It takes mature strength to be affectionate. Dr. Rollo May makes this clear when he writes "... tenderness goes along with strength: one can be gentle as he is strong..."[14]

Affection is love unafraid to let itself be known.

Any man who doubts the persuasive power of kindly affection can have his doubts swept away by the first woman to whom he genuinely gives it!

Here is how Professor Ernest R. Groves encourages the development of this emotion:

In spite of the fact that affection is ordinarily a quiet emotion, it is one of the strongest and one that exalts the life. Affection

---

14 Rollo May, Ph.D., *Man's Search for Himself* (New York: W. W. Norton and Company, Inc., 1953).

encourages the sense of social well-being. It leads to trust, loyalty, and social confidence. It is powerful. . . . Affection, sympathy, and joy deserve positive encouragement. Their development brings on that enrichment of the inner life of the individual which attunes it to the agreeable and elevating experiences of life. The self that possesses them attracts the conditions that make for happiness.[15]

Why is it so essential that we show others that we like them? The plain fact is that most people have such an incredibly low opinion of themselves that they just can't see how anyone could possibly like them. Beneath their outer shells of gaiety and self-confidence lurks a dreadful discouragement toward the person they call "I."

People yearn to believe that you like them, but you as a wise persuader must constantly help them believe that you do. Show them. Make it a special point to show the lady in your life.

Women: What You Can Believe About Men!

You can make yourself an influence over men. But first you need to know how they operate, you should have a grasp of what goes on in the male mind. Use the listed information as tools for persuading that man in your life — or for influencing the man you expect to come your way.

You can always believe that:

1. He wants you to depend upon him.

2. He appreciates your tolerance of his faults.

3. He enjoys a woman who can enjoy herself.

4. He is stubborn at times and knows it.

5. He wants you to be proud of him.

---

15 *Understanding Yourself,* by Ernest R. Groves, Rev. 1949; copyright 1939, 1941 by Emerson Books, Inc. Reprinted by permission of the publishers.

6. He is devoted to the woman who plays fair.

7. He is ambitious toward his career.

8. He often thinks you don't understand him.

9. He can be nicer than you sometimes think.

10. He appreciates your spontaneous kindness.

11. He would rather be comfortable than stylish.

12. He doesn't like to feel inferior.

13. He is more easily persuaded than you imagine.

14. He wants to be thought wise.

15. He often wonders why you act like that.

16. He worries about making mistakes.

17. He falls for sweetness in a woman.

18. He likes to lead the parade.

19. He is attracted to a cheerful woman.

20. He often thinks he is fooling you.

21. He likes a hint of mystery in you.

22. He is not always as confident as he appears.

23. He hopes you admire him.

24. He prefers to think himself as a great lover.

25. He is receptive to your tactful suggestions.

26. He wonders why you cry about it.

27. He can be pretty nice to have around after all.

28. He wants you to ask his opinion.

29. He wants you to meet him halfway.

30. He appreciates and needs your patience.

31. He likes a woman who likes him.

32. He sometimes conveniently exaggerates your faults.

33. He wonders why you never get to the point.

34. He is more bashful toward women than he admits.

35. He needs your subtle encouragement.

36. He doesn't want excessive demands made on him.

37. He needs times to relax from his pressures.

38. He admires grace in a woman.

39. He welcomes your gentleness.

40. He has a lively interest in sex.

Point 10, *He appreciates your spontaneous kindness,* is worthy of an interesting example:

At one time I drove over to a high school in Los Angeles where I had been invited to address one of the student clubs. The young man assigned to escort me to the auditorium was one of those cheerfully talkative boys who fortunately hadn't learned as yet to be shy with strangers. As we cut across the campus he enthused, "Mr. Howard, the nicest thing happened to me yesterday afternoon."

"Tell me about it," I encouraged.

"Well, when I left school I was feeling sort of depressed. I had just been handed lower grades than I expected on my report card. I was wandering toward home, sadly thinking about it, when I came to an intersection. I stopped, of course, to make sure it was safe to cross the street. As I stood there, a low, red convertible swung around the corner in front of me. Behind the wheel was a pretty girl with dark hair and red lips. Know what happened as she passed in front of me? She looked at me and gave me the sweetest, prettiest and kindest smile I have ever had. It was almost as if she had said, 'You're nice. I like you.' You know, Mr. Howard, I walked home in a grateful daze. What a surprise. What a wonderful woman. I'll never forget her. She smiled at me!"

That spontaneous woman, whoever she was, has exerted a lifelong influence upon that young man. All in the space of a few seconds. All because of her voluntary kindness. Just because she smiled. *There* was a charming woman.

In the intercourse of social life, it is by little acts of watchful kindness recurring daily and hourly, it is by words, by tones, by gestures, by looks, that affection is won and preserved. (G. A. Sala)

"The happiness of life may be greatly increased by small courtesies which manifest themselves by tender and affectionate looks, and little acts of attention." (Laurence Sterne)

Let's next look into point 25, *He is receptive to your tactfully-given suggestions.* You ladies might be surprised at how easily you can turn a man in your direction simply by the process of smooth suggestion. I want to tell you an interesting story from the pages of history, quite a remarkable one. It truly illustrates the point:

There was once a young Syrian girl named Iulia Domna. Iulia was a simple peasant girl, but she possessed a magic secret—she knew how a man's mind worked. That gave her a tremendous confidence in dealing with men. In fact, she had such faith in herself that one day she sat down and wrote a persuasive letter to a man. It was mailed not to just any man, but to one occupy-ing the very top of the political world— Septimius Severus, the Roman ruler of France. What was in the note? First of all, a coy suggestion that she would make him a fine wife! Secondly, the spirited Iulia predicted that with her assistance he might rise to even taller stature in the political world.

Septimius was only human, and male human at that. The colos-sal confidence that this mere maiden had in him staggered his mind and delighted his heart. He did the only thing possible: He invited her to the palace to talk things over. That was all it took. They talked about his future. The charming Iulia again suggested that with her at his side he could expect further enrichments of his political fortunes. He took her at her word. Then—what else could he do?—he took her as his bride.

Time passed. Guess who became Emperor of Rome? That's right—Septimius Severus, the former governor. And guess who became the leading lady of the land? Yes, the former peasant girl who once wrote a tactfully-worded note!

Any woman can use the power of subtle suggestion as a means of elevating her position. She *should* use it. It can help advance both herself and the man in her life.

What Is Love?

I once attended a social affair where I and the other guests found ourselves fascinated by the wide varieties of candies set around the rooms. Wherever you went in the home or patio there were dishes filled with delicious chocolates, caramels, bonbons, taffy, butterscotch, and much more. I remarked to a friend that it made an unusually attractive display, then asked him how come. He nodded toward our host and replied, "He owns a candy company."

I'd like this to illustrate that, when all is said and done, the best attractions which any of us can have are our personal qualities, those we own within us. These are the natural confections that attract and appeal to all. If we want to influence others favorably — including the men and women in our lives — we must own and display those very qualities which we yearn for in others.

Foremost among our personal powers is that of love. It is one which we can all take responsibility for, to develop and display. When we do our part we need never fear that we will fail to attract and win those whom we need for a life that is both exciting and comforting. "Love is of all the stimulants the most powerful. It sharpens the wits ... it spurs the will... it intoxicates like wine." (A. H. Edwards)

What is love? Dr. Rollo May offers this definition:

> We define love as *a delight in the presence of the other person and an affirming of his value and development as much as one's own.* Thus there are always two elements to love-that of the worth and good of the other person, and that of one's own joy and happiness in the relation with him.[16]

Why should we love?

Because there is no other way to live happily. Because the human heart always has needed and always will need all the love it can find.

---

16 Rollo May, Ph.D., *Mans Search for Himself* (New York: W. W. Norton and Company, Inc., 1953).

Winning Points For This Chapter

1. You love another best when you understand him. Your understanding of that man or woman is the means by which you naturally influence love in return.

2. Build and maintain realistic attitudes toward the opposite sex. Do not permit an unhappy experience from a past relationship to harm a present one.

3. Have the courage to love and to be loved.

4. Employ the persuasive power of words. You find the other person most charming when you tell him that he is.

5. A man can delight his lady by being skillfully aggressive. Any student of love can please his girl by holding her hand, but it is the advanced lover who thrills her heart by giving that hand an occasional squeeze.

6. Men should remember and practice, "With all women, gentleness is the most persuasive and powerful argument." (Gautier)

7. A woman should never forget that a man is more easily influenced than she may think. Use the suggestions in this book to convince yourself.

8. Any woman who wants to appeal instantly to a man should simply enjoy herself with him. This makes him feel that he is nice to have around —which he may well be.

9. "Caresses, expressions of one sort or another, are necessary to the life of the affections as leaves are to the life of a tree." (Nathaniel Hawthorne)

10. Love is the greatest influence of all... with all... for all.

FACING PEOPLE WITH CONFIDENCE AND ENERGY

The story is told about Julius Caesar who was commanding an expedition of foreign conquest through a mountainous region:

As they reached the top level of a long mountain they saw below them a broad valley. Across the valley was another long mountain. On top of it were the enemy troops, strongly settled in defense position. Caesar glanced at the sun which was descending rapidly into the western horizon. The offensive, the Roman general knew, had to be made before darkness set in. That meant that every man must be placed in attack position at once.

One of Caesar's lieutenants, in charge of messenger pigeons, spoke up, "Sir, we have 500 reserve troops camped 10 miles north. Also, the buglers are waiting at a point 10 miles south. We have only one pigeon left. Shall I send it to call up the troops?"

"No," Caesar replied. "It takes more than men to win battles. Send for the buglers. I need their stirring notes to send my troops charging into the enemy. Inspired action conquers all. Get the buglers here at once."

People are more than willing to follow the man who inspires them to daring action. Just as the bugle blasts energized Caesar's soldiers, so your courage can inspire men and women to follow your lead. Personal heroism is a magnificent necessity for influencing others.

"Confidence is conqueror of men." (Tupper)

As for energy, the classic author Goethe declares, "Energy will do anything that can be done in this world."

No matter what you want out of life you will get it ten times faster by facing people with full confidence and energy. No one really doubts the truth of that; we are all aware of how excellently we perform whenever we throw a courageous and energetic self into the thick of the task. Happily, these two qualities develop each other; as your confidence grows, so does your energy; and your energy has a way of inspiring you with fresh confidence.

The first few chapters of this book have supplied you with a variety of vital techniques for winning your way with others. This chapter adds some music to the words. Or, in mathematical terms it looks like this:

Technique + confidence + energy = victorious social relations.

If you ask, "How do I build more of these powers into my life?" the first step is:

Be a Mind Reader and Be More Confident

Would you handle people with more zeal and certainty if you could read their minds? That's right. You would.

You can turn yourself into a mind reader and quite a skillful one at that. "Every man is a volume, if you know how to read him." (Channing) You enhance your self-assurance enormously once you learn to penetrate the other person's secret thoughts.

How can you do it? Let's consider Lawrence K. who operates a prosperous real estate firm.

He dropped in one afternoon with a challenging problem. "Quite often," he began, "I have trouble sizing up my prospect, I mean, I can't seem to get on to him as quickly and as accurately as is needed. If only I could find some way to deduce quickly the kind of a personality he is, I would know how to persuade him with maximum force. But you know how secretive people usually are; they don't give themselves away very easily. Even when you ask questions that they should gladly answer for their own benefit they have a way of clamming up; for instance, I always try to find out just how much a client wants to invest in his home, but the answer is often evasive. That's the problem. How can I make a prompt appraisal of my man? Is there such a system?"

"There is. And it will give you a surprisingly clear insight into the mind of your man."

"I'm listening."

"Let's illustrate the process. Supposing you walk past a tree and notice a single orange on it. Although you saw only one orange, you know that there must be more oranges somewhere behind the leaves. You realize that one orange indicates more fruit of a like nature." I see.

"Here is the point: By observing a single character trait in the other man you can promptly make a whole series of deductions about his nature as a whole. Just as a certain kind of fruit indicates the presence of other fruit of a similar nature, so does one type of attitude indicate others similar to it. Take, for instance, the attitude of secretiveness that you mentioned. Name a character trait that it allied to extreme secretiveness."

"Fear."

"That's right. Your man may worry that you will try to sell him a more expensive home than he can afford, or maybe he hesitates to admit that he has very little money for a down payment. Let's go on with our deductions. Now that you realize that you have both a secretive and a frightened man in front of you, what else can you logically deduce—in other words, what are some other negative attitudes that accompany there two?"

"Anxiety and tension."

"All right. Now that you know that you have a tense prospect, what can you do as an expert salesman to reduce his tension over buying a house?"

"For one thing, I could assure him that I will take care of as many of the details as possible. Lots of people secretly worry over escrow charges and other financial aspects."

"There you have it. By first observing a single mental trait in your man you have found several others that go with it. That gave you a sound base from which to work at relieving your man's mind. His relief is your persuasion."

As Lawrence steadily practices his mind-reading act he will become a far more effective people-persuader. And so will you if you will do likewise.

Perhaps the greatest value of this method is that it permits you to take the bold initiative in swinging another around to what you want. The other man is not going to come right out and admit that he is anxious over this or worried over that, because it is his desire to give an impression of being confident and at ease. But when you become aware of his actual condition you can take the lead in putting him at ease.

It is an excellent idea to practice your mind-reading act habitually as you go about your daily affairs at home and while doing business. Remember these steps:

1. Observe a dominant characteristic displayed by the other person, perhaps a negative one such as worry, or maybe a positive one such as cheeriness.

2. Deduce other character traits that normally go with it, for instance, a worrisome state would indicate confusion; while a cheerful condition would mean that that person is also more or less receptive to your suggestions.

3. Work at influencing one of his conditions. Try to reduce the anxiety of the worried man. Show the receptive man the many benefits to be won by signing on your dotted line.

Experiment with this for a while. You will be pleasantly surprised at your growing ability to read the other person's mind and character. From that point on it is but a short step toward winning him over.

It's Good to Break the Rules

For many years it was a tradition in the theater that an actor should never turn his back on his audience. Because of that rule no actor or actress ever dared to do so. One evening a certain actor decided to test the validity of the tradition. During one scene in which he was supposed to be gazing upward at the stars in reverence and wonderment, he turned his back on the audience. What happened as a result of the experiment? He uncovered a highly effective dramatic technique that impressed audiences everywhere. Nowadays, actors and actresses follow the new rule with considerable success.

This anecdote introduces you to a vital point concerning your dealings with other people. To face men and women with greater confidence and energy, start breaking some of the traditional rules— of a negative nature—which you may have been following up to now.

You probably have a fairly good idea of your line of action when it comes to handling the people in your life. Think things over until you discover some of the actions and attitudes which seem to be holding you back from full power. Now start breaking the rules.

Here are 10 typical traditions which should be broken and replaced at once:

1.	Old Rule:	Permitting another's mere opinion to influence you.
	New Rule:	*Examine all opinions for actual value.*
2.	Old Rule:	Thinking that you have reached the limit of your power with people.
	New Rule:	*Realize that there are vast and unexplored areas of mastery in dealing with others.*
3.	Old Rule:	Drawing back in dismay when confronted with a baffling problem in persuading people.
	New Rule:	*Work and experiment with the 'problem until the solution finally appears.*
4.	Old Rule:	Waiting and hoping for other people to come to you with good things.
	New Rule:	*Take the initiative in going toward people with exciting ideas for mutual benefit.*
5.	Old Rule:	Expecting too much of people.
	New Rule:	*Permit people to behave pretty much like people.*
6.	Old Rule:	Thinking that the persuasion of people is a hard chore.
	New Rule:	*Know that skill in human relations is a delightful adventure.*
7.	Old Rule:	Spending time with another.
	New Rule:	*Make yourself interesting to the one with whom you spend your time.*
8.	Old Rule:	Permitting gloomy people to distract and discourage you from your declared goals.
	New Rule:	*Keep your attention and intention on the prizes you want from other people.*
9.	Old Rule:	Giving in to anger or upset when a disagreement arises with someone.
	New Rule:	*Honestly and fairly search out the real reason the disagreement upset you as it did.*
10.	Old Rule:	Pretending that you are having a good time because that is what you are expected to do.
	New Rule:	*Have a good time because you are doing what you really want to do.*

Let's see how an official of a travel agency successfully broke and replaced the rule listed at point 3. (This is the one where you valiantly advance toward a solution, rather than give in to dismay.)

This businessman's agency had prepared a booklet which described the exciting adventures awaiting those who engaged their services. It was loaded with appeal for those contemplating a vacation voyage. There were color photographs of the romantic beaches of the South Seas islands. One page described buried pirate's treasure worth $5,000,000 which some lucky traveler just might stumble upon. The booklet's last page described various cruises and tours which the reader might select.

The booklets were set in the lobby of the agency with a sign above them reading TAKE ONE. For some reason or other they were not picked up in quantities that the official had hoped for. Was the time and expense he had put into the booklets going to waste? At first it seemed so. But could something be done about it? He firmly believed so.

After thinking things through he made a simple change in the sign above the booklets. He removed the one reading TAKE ONE and replaced it with another sign with the invitation YOU MAY TAKE ONE.

The results? Almost twice as many visitors took them home, and, of course, that many more became interested in the services offered.

Two little words, but what an impact on people!

Once that official had made up his mind that there *was* a solution to his problem, here is how his mind reasoned its way to success: "The TAKE ONE sign sounds like an order, not like an invitation. It's too cold and abrupt. But its replacement of YOU MAY TAKE ONE conveys a feeling of warmth and cordiality. Everyone responds to an invitation with that much personal friendliness."

Fill in the following black spaces with your own old rules which you intend to break, then add the new ones which guarantee your immediate progress.

1.	Old Rule:
	New Rule:

2.	Old Rule:
	New Rule:

3.	Old Rule:
	New Rule:

4.	Old Rule:
	New Rule:

5.	Old Rule:
	New Rule:

How to Get Rid of Fear of People in Six Seconds

There is the story of little Billy who was told by his mother that his country cousin Peter was coming for a visit. Billy excitedly awaited the day for Peter to arrive. Finally, as the visitor stepped from the train little Billy burst into tears of disappointment.

"Why are you crying?" his astonished mother asked.

"Because," came the sobbing reply, "I thought Peter was a rabbit."

Little Billy set himself up for that disappointment by prejudging the nature of his visitor. And that is something to avoid in all your human contacts. Do not label people when first meeting them. Notice how we have the tendency to do this. We meet someone for the first time and at once we begin to judge them as being "nice" or maybe "not so pleasant" or perhaps as "weak" or maybe as "dangerous" to our welfare.

First impressions are quite often wrong because they are usually based upon our habitual attitudes toward people in general, and not on the present person as he actually is. And once we have made a wrong judgment about someone we force ourselves into wrong acts and attitudes—and away flies our power for persuading them. You may have had the experience of disliking someone at first glance, then later discovering in him a valuable friend. The fact was, he was the very same person all along; it was simply that your attitude toward that person changed.

The point is, do not deliberately adopt any particular attitude toward a person whom you meet for the first time. It often causes confusion and considerable uncertainty. Rather, let the other person reveal himself to you. Once he does so you can handle him realistically and with far more skill and confidence.

If the prejudging of people results in confused interpersonal relations, then how can we look at strangers so as to command them instantly? Here is how to get rid of fear of people *in six seconds.*

Richard B. is a banking official with an important and responsible position. Among other duties, the bank depends upon his ability to create goodwill among those who come in on matters of finance. The bank couldn't have picked a better man for the position, for Richard is one of those smooth and sincere charmers who wins the respect of male clients and the confidence of the ladies.

A natural-born charmer? Richard himself would be the first to deny any special favors from nature when it came to handing out captivating personalities.

"I was just as shy and awkward as anyone," he admitted. "That is, until I learned a secret that changed the entire course of my life. It also helped double my salary."

"Go ahead," I urged. "Tell me the secret."

"I call it the Think Back system. It's been my own special method for ridding myself of fear of people almost instantly. It never fails."

"How about some details?"

"Take a typical afternoon a few years ago when an important executive of a fifty-million dollar industry called in for my counsel. Maybe he wanted information on the financing of an expansion program. Well, at that time I was a bit jittery at the idea of handling such an important man. You know how it goes; you hope to make a good impression, you want to make sure that you satisfy his needs, and so on. Let me tell you that there's nothing like being scared for making you act like a complete idiot. I fumbled and fooled and managed to get by without fouling up the deal but that was about all. I wasn't calm or confident or resourceful—I was just plain ill at ease, or call it scared. I knew I had to do something about it and quick. I did. The Think Back technique did it."

"How does it work?"

"It's very simple. Have you ever noticed that the better you know someone the less frightening he becomes to you? He gets more human, perhaps a bit faulty; you get to see him through the eyes of reality, not through those of a blown-up imagination. As he becomes more human, you become less frightened. That, in a nutshell, is the secret. Whenever I got overly impressed with someone I began to Think Back to a *previous* person who used to scare me. I thought of how my timidity vanished as we got to know each other better. Then I pictured the man in front of me as *already* humanized. I got to musing as to how often he lost his temper in the highway traffic and wondered if he sometimes worried whether or not his children would turn out okay. Soon I was at ease with that man, and he with me. It had taken me about three seconds to Think Back to previous people who had once scared me and about three seconds more to remember that this man in front of me was also pretty much human. That's how to get rid of fear of people in six seconds."

Anyone can face other people with full confidence and energy. All it takes is the retraining of mental attitudes. The Dutch philosopher Spinoza declared, "I saw that all the things I feared . . . had nothing good or bad in them save in so far as the mind was affected by them." Whenever you find yourself timid or hesitant, try to find some small opening for retraining your attitudes.

One man who was hesitant about offering his opinions when with others demanded the following retraining exercise of himself: At least three times during a social occasion he would break the silence by speaking up. He never tried to say anything especially clever or of earth-shaking significance; the whole idea was to get used to hearing himself say something, say anything. In time he found himself forgetting that it was a retraining program; he began to speak up naturally, spontaneously, and with far more talent than he thought possible.

Familiarity breeds confidence. We all know this to be true when it comes to learning to drive an automobile or acquiring skill in sports. The same principle of familiarity can rapidly build more confidence and energy into your social relations.

Set your mind aside. Don't think. Make contact. Repeatedly. Watch fear flee!

How to Keep Yourself Excited

There was once a Pennsylvania businessman who consistently asked himself the question, "What do I want?"

The answer he consistently heard from himself was, "I want to sell lots of candy to lots of people."

That answer kept him on fire with confidence and energy. It gave him power and drive for plunging through so-called obstacles and setbacks. He wanted to sell lots of candy to lots of people. That was what he wanted from the world of people. Anything else—especially failure—was brushed aside as a triviality.

His confidence and energy made him a millionaire.

The whole thing started in a small rented building in Philadelphia. The venturesome candymaker worked over his stove and kettles to turn out penny candies for the neighborhood children. So many youngsters skipped into his shop that he soon had to move to a larger building. It looked like success was just around the corner. But something happened. He ran out of working capital. That ended the candymaker's success for the moment, but it didn't dim his confidence and energy. He still knew what he wanted—to sell lots of candy to lots of people.

Again he plunged into business. His confections were sold to both retail and wholesale outlets. Things looked good. But again he ran into financial difficulties. The demands from the sugar refineries for payment outran his collections from his own slow paying customers. That ended his participation in that phase of his career, but it didn't end his dream of persuading lots of people to buy lots of his candy.

The excited candymaker finally settled upon Lancaster, Pennsylvania as the headquarters for another major venture. He and the four employees of the Lancaster Caramel Company were soon turning out tasty candy that sold by the truckloads. So enthusiastic was the public welcome to his sweets that the company was forced to expand to cover a city block. The number of employees swelled to two thousand. Finally, an offer came from a rival candy company. The head of the Lancaster Caramel Company was shown a certified check for $1,000,000. Would he sell for that figure? He would. He did.

But our enthusiastic candymaker was not ready to retire from business. He had made money, lots of money, but he still wanted to sell lots of candy to lots of people. He wondered how he could persuade even more people to taste his sweets. In a small way he began to experiment with candy bars made of milk chocolate. The very first time his customers tasted them they were persuaded to buy lots of them. Business prospered amazingly.

Today, the influence of that candymaker is felt every day by millions of people all over the world. To put it mildly, lots of people buy lots of his candy. His name? You have heard it: *Milton Hershey.* His business? The Hershey Chocolate Corporation of Hershey, Pennyslvania.

Milton Hershey faced his public with full confidence and energy because he knew what he wanted. He won what he wanted.

What do you want from the world of people? Let your desire inspire you. Release it fully. Never mind what you *think about* your goal. Concentrate solely on the goal itself. That is how you win it.

If you know what you want from people, what next? What else can you do to insure success? That is what we next take up.

I often ask successful people whether they have particular techniques which keep them excited toward their plans. One man, a junior executive in the meat-packing industry, explained his secret system for pushing his programs of people-persuasion:

> Whenever I feel tempted to slack off in my efforts I ask myself whether I want to cheat myself. That is exactly what I do whenever I give in to dismay or indifference. Since I don't want to miss out on the best of life, I come alive fast. Off I plunge into a fresh adventure for winning people.
>
> Here is how I organize my enthusiasm. At the end of each month I write down its name on the top of a slip of paper. If the month happens to be January I list all the good things that came my way during that period as a result of my efforts. For example, I might list the name of a new business client worth an extra 50 dollars per month in commissions. Maybe I write down the name of a clubwoman who offered to give my company some newspaper publicity. Down go all the names of people who helped promote my business life or my personal affairs.
>
> Next I take another slip of paper and head it with the new month, in this case, February. Under it I add nothing; there is blank space only. I set the two slips side by side and consider them carefully. Because of my energetic persistence I have won all those valuable prizes in January. Had I not persisted, or had I slackened my effort, I would surely have cheated myself of some of them. I ask myself right then and there whether I want a blank page at the end of the present month of February or whether I want progress. Let me tell you, when I see the cold facts of what my persistence does for me there is no stopping me from plunging ahead in February also.
>
> At the end of each month I show myself what I won during that period. That little reminder keeps me speeding forward in my

people-persuading programs during March and April and all the rest of the year. Who wants to be left out? Not I!

The feeling of missing out on something is one of the busiest of all emotions (but one of the least admitted, for people like to put up a front of being contented). This emotion can work for you or against you, depending upon what you do with it. "Strong impulses are but another name for energy." (John Stuart Mill). Here is a perfect opportunity for taking an apparently negative feeling and turning it into a constructive force that carries you forward.

Decide right now that you are *not* going to be left out of all the riches that await you in better human relations. That decision will keep you confident and will charge you with new energy. And it just so happens that your confidence and your energy are two reliable people-persuaders all by themselves.

Dynamic Ideas to Remember

1. Your energetic confidence is the magnet that attracts instant attention and maintains constant respect from others.

2. "The great characteristic of men of active genius is a sublime self-confidence. . ." (E. P. Whipple)

3. Throw all your available enthusiasms into your people-persuading plans. You will discover that the more you spend your energies the more you have.

4. Practice the techniques for becoming a mind reader. Knowing what is on the other person's mind is a major secret for commanding him.

5. Dare to break away from all negative attitudes that restrict your progress with people. Example: Abandon the notion that human attitudes cannot be changed and
improved. You, for one, can change them.

6. Practice the Think Back technique supplied in this chapter.

7. Get closer acquainted with people or situations which baffle you. Familiarity breeds confidence.

8. Definition of courage: The willingness to do some new thing today that you didn't do yesterday.

9. Repeatedly remind yourself of what you want from the world of people. Your very desire inspires confidence and determination. "What we seek, we shall find..." (Emerson)

10. Make up your mind that you will not cheat yourself out of richer relations with people. Any man who thinks he has to be left out, just thinks so.

CLEVER STEPS FOR GETTING AROUND DIFFICULT PEOPLE

As we all know from experience, there are some difficult and unreasonable people in this world. But we should also know at once that the clever commander can really quite easily turn them into allies and friends and customers.

The first thing to do is to abandon any negative attitudes we may have toward problem-people. Always consider them as interesting challenges to your powers of persuasion, never as people to be disliked or avoided.

> Just before the invasion of Sicily by the Allied armies in World War II, the commanders in charge of the operation faced a serious problem in the weather. The skies and seas were stormy. And it could get worse. The commanders knew it was going to be a tough enough task to beat back the enemy troops once they met them on the fortified beaches—to have to first fight their way through the raging seas doubled the difficulty.

> Yet the plunge had to be made. There was a war to win. The commanders realized that there was nothing they could do about the weather itself, but something *could* be done with

their viewpoint toward it. So that is what they changed. They make up their minds to turn the seeming problem into an active force in their behalf. Reasoning that the enemy would not expect an attack during the storm, the Allies lunged toward Sicily. The enemy troops rolled back in shock and eventual defeat. Sicily was won.

Likewise, you can work with people who have stormy or difficult natures and win them over. So from now on, take the attitude that they are seemingly difficult to persuade or to help. This fresh viewpoint plunges you into the right kind of action that wins the day.

Also, we should realize from the very start that no man or woman ever really *wants* to be difficult or unkind or hostile. He acts that way because he knows no better way to act. He is a problem to others because he is first of all a problem to himself. He is a person of painful contradictions, for while he knows that his hostility is self-destructive he just doesn't know how to free himself *from himself.* The problem-person does not know that it really *is* possible to live a happy life. Finally, the difficult person suffers plenty of pain from his confusion; you can be sure of that.

The fact that no man really wants to be a difficult person is high tribute to the basic goodness within him, but which he is unable to find. If you ever want to restore your faith in human nature, just remember that every person earnestly desires to be better than he is. He just doesn't know what to do or where to turn or how to proceed.

So-called difficult people are pretty much like the rest of us: they want to be wanted. They like your appreciation and your patience. They hope for your understanding. They have an even greater need for these things, and that is why you have more of an opportunity for persuading and helping them.

I am thinking of a man who is now an officer with a large chain of supermarkets. It took him about one-half the usual time to advance from clerical duties to his own private office. He owes his success to his unusual ability in persuading difficult people to become non-difficult. Whenever an irate shopper complains of injury incurred on company property he knows how to smooth things over. If an employee comes to him with a pressing personal problem he comes up with the right answers.

In other words, this man has made unusual progress in his career because of his unusual ability to handle people with severe problems. He knows that they require special handling. He also knows that the more difficult a person makes himself the more easily you can win him over — providing you handle him skillfully.

Take the individual with an extremely suspicious mind. Offhand you would think that his suspiciousness prevents him from being influenced by anyone. The exact opposite is the truth. He is much more easily persuaded than you might imagine, for this type of person believes almost everything; his suspicion is a sort of negative faith.

Your bold and confident approach will win over this kind of person. Not having too much judgment of his own, not knowing what to really believe, he willingly accepts the conclusions of someone with lots of confidence and decisiveness. He *wants* to be persuaded, so give him what he needs. He will not only come your way but thank you for it.

How to Win Over a Frightened Person

Every time you set out to persuade a man to your way of thinking you must take into account the enormously powerful emotion of fear. Why? Because the vast majority of people are influenced, to one extent or another, by their fears. This they don't like. If you will become a counter-influence you will be a highly welcome person wherever you go. An entire program for mastering and commanding people could be based on this idea alone. Because people are afraid they yearn constantly for relief from that painful emotion.

Remember that fear and hostility go hand-in-hand. A man who is frightened is apt to be angry and self-defensive. Also remember that you must never take his hostility personally; he is not really attacking you, he is simply releasing his pressures on a handy individual.

Fear reveals itself in lots of ways. The critical person often attempts to cover his own fear of criticism by being the first to strike. The man who can't make up his mind is influenced by the fear of making a mistake in judgment. The woman who keeps telling you how many men are chasing after her is sounding her alarm at being chased by none. The so-called lazy person may be so haunted by the fear of failure that he won't even try to succeed. The person who is constantly indignant at the morals of others is giving away his fearful envy of not having as good a time as those who shock him.

When dealing with any kind of a difficult person, always assume that he is afraid of something, for he is. He may call it by a noble name; for instance, a customer may tell you that he is a wise buyer who likes to consider all the angles before deciding, but it is your duty as an expert in human nature to realize that his hesitation is really due to some worry he has about your product. Knowing this you can assure him that your product is really a time-saver or that it will definitely pay for itself within a few days or that it will certainly simplify his work.

A person whom you are trying to influence will rarely come right out and admit to you that he is afraid of this or that. It is typical of human nature that none of us like to admit our timidities to ourselves, much less to another. You should try to identify the other person's particular uncertainty, tactfully, of course. Probe around, make it easy for him to come out with his objections. Sometimes it is enough to ask casually if there is some point which he would like cleared up. This often gives him encouragement enough to come out with his hidden timidity or problem. You can take it from there.

How can you free your man of his anxieties? That is what you need to find out. In many cases it is best not to try and sell your product or program itself, but show him how its use will free him from some underlying anxiety. Once this is done, the sale is assured. Notice how freedom-from-fear is offered by the advertisers: Put our safe tires on your car and you need never worry about a blow-out. Eat our low-calorie foods and rest assured you won't gain weight. Buy our insurance and relieve your mind of financial stress.

So show the other man how your program will relieve his mind. Let him breathe easier. Promise and deliver freedom. Release him from his inner anxieties. Do this and you do him a favor he will remember.

Check-List of Major Fears

Let's next go through a list of some of the commonplace anxieties and worries. By clearly identifying them we become more skilled in helping others.

People are afraid of:

1. being rejected and unwanted.
2. the new and the unknown.
3. inability to break unwanted habits.
4. losing a loved one.
5. criticism and disapproval.
6. boredom.
7. financial insecurity.
8. appearing foolish.
9. failing to attract others.
10. effort without reward.
11. loneliness.
12. being cheated out of a full life.
13. not living up to expectations.
14. loss of any kind.
15. invasion of privacy.
16. heartache and of getting hurt.
17. being taken advantage of.
18. personal passions and feelings.
19. weakness and inadequacy.
20. losing out in love and sex.

Let's go into a few details on *points 5,10,15, 20:* Active in every man is the dread of criticism and disapproval.

If he interprets your efforts at persuasion as an attack upon his present way of doing things, he is bound to stubbornly resist you. You can get around him by completely ignoring his present inadequate action and by showing him how its opposite — a positive action — will enrich him. A sales-manager called a meeting for the purpose of turning his salesmen's energies into more constructive channels, for some of them were wasting too much time in trivial paper-work. He started out by complimenting their devotion to detail, then suggested they detail their plans for expanded action in the field. The salesmen were not even aware that they were being persuaded to strengthen their work habits. That sales-manager won them completely by side-stepping their sensitivity to direct criticism.

Look at *point 10:* Most people have done so many things without getting something from their efforts that they are a bit skeptical of tackling new plans that may be suggested to them. This means that you should keep your man excited over the forthcoming rewards he can expect from his cooperation. Convince him that his investment will return a clear-cut profit — perhaps financially, maybe in increased popularity, perhaps in an improved personal appearance. Impress him with his need for doing something *today* in order to possess a superior *tomorrow.*

> The story is told about an expedition struggling upward toward one of the unconquered peaks in the Swiss Alps. Halfway up the men began to doubt that their strenuous efforts would pay off. The more they thought about it the more reluctant they were to follow their captain's orders. But their leader was something of a psychologist as well as a mountaineer. He held a hand toward the towering peak while declaring, "Look where you'll be. On top of the world!" By repeating that persuasive promise, he convinced his men of the glory that awaited them on top of the mountain. That was enough to spur them upward to final conquest.

Let's see what we have in *point 15:* Everyone has his private life and his secret thoughts which he wants to keep from prying eyes.

That is his right; privacy is a basic human need. No matter how much you know about the other person, don't let him know that you know. He is not going to thank you for violating his private world. As that wise Frenchman La Rochefoucauld once wrote, "We love to see through others, but we dislike being seen through." Whenever you are trying to talk another into going your way, do not accuse him of being afraid or timid or weak. He may actually be that way, but your business is to keep it to yourself while working at reducing his fears. La Rochefoucauld again remarks, "It is exceedingly clever to know how to hide your cleverness."

In *point 20* we see an emotion which constantly and anxiously paces back and forth within people: the fear of losing out in love and sex. Everyone wants to be loved and almost everyone doubts that he is. Typical of this deep yearning are the touching lines from a French drama in which the heroine appeals to her *paramour,* "Please tell me that you love me. It doesn't have to be true; you don't have to mean it. I just want to hear you say that you love me."

This whole book could be summed up by saying that the most influential force on earth is that of love: *love* in the form of tenderness and of affection; *love* as patience and as the willingness to take another's unkindness without bitterness; *love* as permitting one to be difficult or unreasonable because you understand that he or she knows no other way.

Love is still the incredible force that conquers all, including fear. "It is a wonderful subduer — this need of love, this hunger of the heart." (George Eliot)

Here are the three main ideas to remember from preceding pages:

1. Think of difficult people as frightened and anxious people, for that is what they really are. The more of a problem they present to you the more anxiety they possess — and hence the greater their need for your calm reassurance and patient assistance.

2. You can turn a man's stubbornness into cooperation by lowering his level of fear. Whatever you are trying to sell or put across,

this system works for you. At what point does a person say yes to your ideas? It is really quite simple. He goes along with you when he is no longer dominated by a fear of the consequences of his agreement.

3. Remember that unreasonable people are not as hopeless as they appear to be. They are like messages written with secret ink — warm them up a bit and they shine through, especially for you. Listen to these cheering words from a noted authority on human behavior, Dr. Karen Horney:

My own belief is that man has the capacity as well as the desire to develop his potentialities and become a decent human being ... I believe that man can change and go on changing .. ,[17]

Quick Methods for Handling Negative People

You are about to be assisted by going through a list of 30 commonplace moods and attitudes. They are the kind that you run into frequently when dealing with other people, and they are more or less negative in character. Each listed mood is followed by a swift system for handling the other person and for helping yourself. Use this list constantly; don't hesitate to employ repeatedly the offered systems in your daily contacts at work or in the home or wherever you meet people.

Most importantly — and never forget this — you can always use the other person's very negativity as a lever for tilting him in your direction.

When the other person is:

1.   *Quarrelsome:* Let him quarrel while you calmly figure out a way to get what you want.

2.   *Silent:* Draw him out with questions. Find out what is on his mind, then take it from there.

---

17 Karen Homey, M.D., *Our Inner Conflicts* (New York: W. W. Norton and Company, Inc., 1945).

3. *Timid:* Take the initiative in assuring him of your good will and helpfulness.

4. *Burdensome:* Don't permit others to constantly unload all their troubles on you. You were not placed here to save the world.

5. *Boastful:* He needs reassurance of his own self-worth. Build it wherever possible.

6. *Threatening:* Quietly refuse to accept his threatening *attitude* as an *actual* threat.   Another's threat has no power to hurt you unless you think it does.

7. *Unenthusiastic:* Let your own enthusiasm fire him up. Everyone responds to enthusiasm because everyone really wants more of it.

8. *Prying:* Insist upon keeping your private life private.

9. *Domineering:* Listen to what he *tells* you to do. Find a way to do what you *want* to do.

10. *Weak:* Show consideration but not prolonged sympathy, for that encourages weakness.   You are kindest to a weak person when you help him to be strong.

11. *Boring:* Ask yourself why you ever got mixed up with him in the first place.

12. *Inefficient:* Parade the rewards of efficiency before him. That will make him want to sharpen himself.

13. *Hateful:* Feel sorry that he is not as happy as you are. Hatred and happiness never go around together.

14. *Critical:* Congratulate yourself. The man who constantly criticizes you is telling you how important you are to him. You have his attention and respect.

15. *Self-righteous:* Take a deep sigh and hope that some day he may be honest enough to enjoy being as faulty as everyone else.

16. *Frightened:* Help him to face squarely the event, idea, or situation which frightens him. Fear exists only when there is a turning away from the feared thing.   You cannot fear reality, you can fear only what you *wrongly think* is real.

17. *Hesitant:* Act with confidence and authority. He needs a strong person to throw off his doubts.

18. *Demanding:* First, calmly tell him that you can do just so much and no more.   Second, do all you reasonably can and make not the slightest attempt to do more.

19. *Worried:* Point out to him that his problems need not be permanent — not if he takes the proper attitude that they need not be permanent.

20. *Touchy:* Treat him tactfully, but under no circumstances permit a touchy person to intimidate you. Intimidation is his subtle and childish weapon which you must absolutely refuse to tolerate.

21. *Stubborn:* Don't try to force him to your way by a frontal attack. Be wise, be smooth, be clever.

22. *Impractical:* Prove to him that his way of doing things is not getting him the results he really wants.   Point out that right actions always produce right results.

23. *Bitter:* Let him be bitter because he doesn't have what he wants. You go out and daringly get what you want.

24. *Unreasonable:* Be strong enough not to return his un reasonableness. He may not admit it, but he will admire it.

25. *Confused:* Tell him that the way out of confusion need not be a sad task but a light-hearted and interesting adventure. It *can* be if he will simply let it be.

26. *Insolent:* Be patient but make it ever so clear that he is not to mistake your patience for weakness.

27. *Gloomy:* Tell him that he can live that way if he wants to, but it's not for you. Remind him that cheeriness is man's natural state.

28. *Irresponsible:* Refuse to take on the duties that belong to another. It is not noble to help those who won't help themselves; it is a sheer loss to both of you.

29. *Angry:* Detach your emotions from him. Cleverly set your calm mind at work to winning your way.

30. *Unkind:* Look at him and wonder why he tortures him self so.

What to Do When Things Go Wrong

If nothing ever goes wrong in your dealings with people, or if you never run into awkward social situations, then you will not need to read this section. But if you think there are areas where you can sharpen your persuasiveness — especially with problem-people — then we can explore together some punchy pointers for expanding your successes.

Whenever a tough challenge arises, or whenever your persuasion-programs are not speeding ahead as rapidly as you wish, employ the following principles:

1. ALWAYS STICK TO WHAT YOU WANT FROM A PROBLEM-PERSON, WHILE IGNORING THE WAY HE BEHAVES

Don't permit your personal feelings toward a difficult person to throw you off the track. Make up your mind that the only important thing is winning your way. Personal feelings like pride, indignation, impatience, and touchiness have absolutely no place in your efforts at persuading another. What we are saying is that you should never permit another's unpleasantness or stubbornness to weaken your purpose. You want something from someone? Good. Go after that and go after that exclusively. This sort of fixed determination is what gave greatness to George Washington. During the American Revolution he was often surrounded by obstinate and wearisome people. He was wise enough to ignore their negative personalities in order to draw upon their knowledge and experience. That wise character trait helped Washington achieve his goal of American independence.

2. CONSTANTLY STUDY THE PROBLEM-PERSON

One of the simplest forces for building your personal power is that of an observing attitude toward those who make things hard. Never resent them; always use them. Carefully study their behavior; it teaches you so much: The ignorant man teaches you the value of knowledge; the opinionated person proves to you the need for an open mind; the withdrawn individual makes clear the need for a daring and outgoing personality. Whenever you see a negative character trait in another, let it spur you toward its opposite.

Another reason why you should not resent thorny people is because they tend to be the most loyal of all once you convert them to your cause. Because they are often rejected or ignored by so many others they stick like glue to the person who accepts and likes them. And this is as good a place as any to repeat one of those oh-so-simple-and-yet-so-profound truths about persuasion: To influence anyone at all, first do your part toward influencing him to like you. Quite often that is all you have to do. Everyone likes to do things for people who like them. That is why the pointers in Chapter 5 are worth gold to you.

3. YOUR TACT WILL WIN YOUR OBJECTIVE

The boss watched his secretary run into the office and throw off her coat. Rushing to the typewriter, she flopped down to pound away furiously. The boss glanced at his watch, then smiled kindly as he spoke to her, "Congratulations, Miss Miller; this is the earliest you've been late."

That is a humorous introduction to that golden quality we call *tact*. If you have never thought of tactfulness as an instrument of persuasion, start doing so now. Whether you call it tact or diplomacy or politeness or social skill, you need it if you want others to enjoy being led by you. As familiar as it is, tact is often overlooked as a method for mastering people. Perhaps that's because it operates quietly unnoticed — and that is its secret of success.

Tact is a perfect example of a secret passage which we read about in Chapter 2. It wins over the other person before he knows what is going on—and when he does discover how you've won him, he likes it.

When dealing with a difficult person, perhaps one who is angry or childish, try to make him see what his unreasonable attitude is costing him. Gently point out his loss in money or in popularity or in happiness or whatever else it might be. At the time he may pretend he doesn't care, but you can be sure that his natural self-interest will make him think twice. As we saw in earlier pages, if there is anything a human being dislikes, it is the missing out on something he *could* have had. With a dash of tact you can keep his childish pride at a minimum and his desire for self-gain at maximum.

Talent is something, but tact is everything. It is the interpreter of all riddles, the surmounter of all difficulties, the remover of all obstacles. (W. P. Sargill)

Your Clever Steps in Review

1. Always think of a problem-person as an exciting challenge to your powers of persuasion. Every time you win one of them you strengthen yourself.

2. Remember that the difficult man or woman has a deep need for your patience and understanding and kindness. Supply these and you help him to help himself.

3. Bear in mind that fear is a constantly experienced emotion. Find ways to reduce the other person's anxieties.

4. You will never find a surer way to influence another person than to like him and let him know that you do.

5. The other person will give the nod to your program when he is no longer afraid of the consequences of his agreement.

6. Constantly employ the 30 quick methods for handling negative people.

7. When dealing with a hostile or unpleasant person, go after what you want and forget your own prides and sensitivities.

8. Never resent those who make it hard on you. Study them. They are living lessons in how not to live.

9. Don't strain yourself in trying to get along with unreasonable people. Your first duty is to keep your own peace of mind.

10. Practice tact. It is the smooth bullet that hits the target.

Chapter

How to Get Other People to Promote Your Interests

There was the wife who worriedly told her husband, "William, I'm worried about our little Tommy."

Asked Dad, "Why? What's he done?"

"Instead of doing his yard work he gets someone else to do it for him. I'm afraid he has no ability to work things out for himself."

"Ability?" Dad delightedly exclaimed. "Why, that boy has *executive* ability."

One of the surest signs of a successful leader is the ability to get others to promote the common interests—which include the leader's interests also.

History is rich with examples of men who climbed to the top of their respective worlds by surrounding themselves with able lieutenants who helped carry out their programs. George Washington was assisted by Benjamin Franklin and Alexander Hamilton. Thomas Edison and Henry Ford surrounded themselves with top-rank scientists and inventors.

Never try to do too much all by yourself. Look around for those who can do you some good. Interdependence is a law of life and one fully employed by wise and resourceful leaders. Self-dependence is absolutely necessary, but this does not at all mean that you must exclude others; it means that you are so sure-minded that you know that others can and will promote your interests. The man who withdraws excessively from other people betrays his lack of trust in both himself and others.

Seek to add valuable people to your life. This means that you should invest in a personal plan for making fresh contacts and for enriching your present ones. Try the following pointers for better contacts:

1.   Know exactly what you want from it.

2.   Make varied contacts for your specific purpose.

3.   Ask the contact itself to suggest mutual profit.

4.   Work at making one contact lead to another.

5.   Find ways to enrich a present association.

6.   Discover how others add valuable people.

7.   Develop new ways for meeting people.

8.   Circulate among valuable people.

Along with this, remember to work steadily at making *yourself* a valuable person. This enables your various contacts to recognize you as such. Like attracts like, success appeals to success. I want to tell you a remarkable story that illustrates this truth:

John J. Pershing was born in Laclede, Missouri. The son of a railroad worker, he had no special advantages to help him, yet he managed to get into West Point by competitive examination. After graduation he went into action against Apache warriors and later commanded his men in the Spanish-American War. Came the Philippine Insurrection and the efficient John J. Pershing was given command of an expedition against the savage Moros. His expert leadership caught the eye of a prominent person—no less than President Theodore Roosevelt. During the Russo-Japanese War the increasingly-valuable Pershing was sent to Manchuria as an observer. His report back to Washington, D. C. was so brilliantly prepared that he once more made a profound impression upon President Roosevelt.

At this time he was known as Captain Pershing.

But he had made himself valuable to another valuable person.

That is why Captain Pershing was promoted to the rank of Brigadier General John J. Pershing.

In one of the most spectacular promotions in the military history of the United States, President Roosevelt jumped Pershing over the head of 862 senior officers.

Pershing's value as a soldier brought him additional fame when he pursued and dispersed Pancho Villa and his bandits below the Mexican border. This skillful action caught the eye of another valuable person—President Woodrow Wilson. John J. ("Black Jack") Pershing climaxed his valuable career by serving as Commander-in-Chief of the American Expeditionary Force in World War I.

To summarize: you can get other people to promote your interests by becoming valuable to them. Therefore, become more and more valuable *yourself* while contacting other people of value. Such a system just can't miss. States Professor Harry Overstreet:

> It is good news that our life can grow in power and happiness as it links itself productively to life other than our own: through willed knowledge, through responsibility, through grace and clarity of words, through empathetic feeling, through sexual understanding, through philosophic grasp.[18]

18 H. A. Overstreet, *The Mature Mind* (New York: W. W. Norton and Company, Inc., 1949).

Establish an Agreeable Atmosphere

You have the power to set the kind of atmosphere you want. And the kind you want is that which induces others to promote your interests.

One of two things always happens whenever you make contact with another person:

1. *You* establish the general atmosphere that *you* want.

2. *He* sets the scene according to *his* wishes.

If you take instant charge of the atmosphere, you are far more likely to walk away with what you want. To state it in reverse, if you lose control of the situation you are also likely to lose out as far as your purpose is concerned.

By *atmosphere* we mean the over-all emotional and mental climate between and surrounding two people. It also includes the attitudes and moods of both parties. A board meeting of an industrial corporation would function best when dominated by an atmosphere of alertness and efficiency. If your objective is to persuade voters to cast their ballots for you, the atmosphere of enthusiasm and excitement would help turn the trick. The correct way to calm down an angry or upset person would be to establish an atmosphere of quiet patience.

How important is it to set the right mood? Extremely. The moviemakers know it. That is why a mystery story may open with shuddery music and storm-drenched castle perched on the edge of the cliff. It is why they introduce you to a musical show by bombarding you with peppy tunes and lively actions.

At this point I want to pass on to you a truth about human nature that may surprise you. It will also enable you to magically establish and control the atmosphere of all your meetings with other people.

The surprising fact is this: People often do not know what kind of an atmosphere is supposed to be "correct" for an occasion. Consequently they wait to see how others are acting and reacting. They then follow along according to what is supposed to be "proper" or "natural." A few days ago I was invited to a party. Because of a previously planned business appointment I arrived an hour late. As I walked up to the door I expected to hear noises that sounded like a party. Instead, as I entered, it sounded like and looked like a prayer meeting. Everyone was sitting stiffly around the room engaged in nervous and embarrassed small talk. All were waiting for someone to set a lively mood, (which the rest would have immediately joined). I felt like tossing a bomb into the center of the room just to loosen things up.

You see, people are afraid to take the lead in establishing a lively and relaxed atmosphere for fear of doing or saying the wrong thing, or maybe because their shyness compels them to remain inconspicuous. Not being sure of the "right" things to do, they play it safe by doing nothing.

What an opportunity for the daring personality!

If you will boldly and tactfully take charge of any situation which presents itself, you can turn it into whatever is best for both you and the other people concerned. You will have instant command over everyone within range of the atmosphere you have created. As an extra bonus, they will be grateful to you for showing them how to act.

In all human contacts there operates what might be called the *Law of Similar Response*. This simply means that other people will respond to your approach in a like manner. If you are gloomy, that's the way they will feel; if you are gay, their spirits tend to soar. The French novelist Victor Hugo explains how this law operates in a love affair: "The first symptom of true love in a man is timidity, in a girl it is boldness. The two sexes have a tendency to approach, and each assumes the qualities of the other/"

It will help you to develop agreeable atmospheres by recalling the childhood game of Follow the Leader. You remember the simple rules: The leader takes the foremost position in line and walks around the room or yard, while climbing over obstacles or making various kinds of gestures. In order to remain in the game, the others must obediently imitate the leader's actions.

Let's employ Mr. A. and Mr. B. to illustrate the differences between the man who establishes an agreeable atmosphere and the man who carelessly lets himself get absorbed by whatever emotional climate he happens to run into.

Whenever Mr. A. wants someone to do something for him, he takes personal responsibility for setting a background of relaxation, friendliness, sincerity . . . Mr. B., on the other hand, fails in his mission because he doesn't prepare a setting agreeable to the other man.

When Mr. A. wants to impress another with the serious need for his program, he seriously supplies good reasons why it should be supported . . . but Mr. B. fails to present facts to back up his stand.

Whenever Mr. A. meets a stranger, he walks up and speaks to him promptly and confidently . . . Mr. B. waits for the other man to take the initiative.

If Mr. A. wishes to establish a cheery and relaxed atmosphere, he acts cheery himself . . . Mr. B. remains sober-faced, while wondering why everyone is sober-faced to him.

Whenever Mr. A. wishes another person to work faster, he sets an example by acting and speaking with full-speed enthusiasm . . . Mr. B. cannot influence anyone to greater effort because he fails personally to set the proper pace.

Any time Mr. A. wants others to have confidence in him, he establishes the atmosphere of confidence by acting decisively and with self-assurance . . . Mr. B. does nothing more than hope that others have confidence in him.

In other words, Mr. A. *deliberately* creates the setting that will cause the other person to respond favorably . . . Mr. B. sits around and lets others take control, often even making himself the victim of negative control.

How do you take charge of the atmosphere? No mystery. You just step up and do it. Command comes to the man with the daring to take it!

Recently I witnessed a delightful example of this while a guest at a friend's home in the countryside. My host was trying to persuade his pretty wife to swim with us in their newly built pool. Having some timidity toward the water, she doubtfully shook her head. With a happy grin on his face her husband went to work on her with appeals like these: "You'll be the prettiest girl on the waves ... I can hardly wait to have you in the water . . . Think of all the fun you'll have."

That established an agreeable atmosphere for her.   She soon joined us in the water.

Remember to take the initiative in setting the favorable atmosphere that you want. That is how to reap its benefits. This is one of the magic powers which you have for mastering and commanding people.

Why You Should Let Others Serve You

Listen to what that brilliant French observer of human nature, La Rochefoucauld, has to say about human preference:

"We prefer being with people we can do things for, rather than being with people who do things for us."

Why do you suppose that we like to do things for others? And why do you imagine that other people like to do favors for us?

It's not really difficult to understand. We have already seen that everyone has a deep yearning to be wanted and desired, to be called upon and asked, to feel needed and necessary.

How does the other person fulfill these constant cravings?

Largely by doing things for you.

Whenever anyone does you a favor or gives you a helping hand, he enhances his own feelings of self-worth. The more he is able to serve you the better he feels toward both himself and you.

The plain fact is, the other person not only wants to serve your interests but his very own personal happiness depends upon it to a major degree. Psychologists have long known that the unhappiest people are those who feel useless and unwanted, while those who pass joyous days are those who have found themselves of help to others.

One of the strangest facts about human thinking is that a man knows that he needs other people desperately, but fails to realize that other people need him with equal intensity. This idea is worth thinking through until its enormous implications stir you to aggressive action. When you realize how much other people need to do things for you, great things begin to happen. Emperor Julius Caesar once declared, "No music is so charming to my ear as the requests of my friends."

You enrich both yourself and the other person when you permit him to do things for you. That is a primary rule to remember whenever you wish to persuade other people to promote your interests.

It may strike you as somewhat amusing, but the question, "What can I do for you?" is often not nearly as effective as the silently asked, "What can you do for me?"

Exactly how do we go about permitting others to serve us?

By request.

That's all. Just ask them.

Not necessarily by a directly spoken request, but by the tactful suggestion, and by pointing out the mutual benefits that will result from their agreement. One request like this produced one of the greatest songs ever written in the United States.

One Saturday evening many years ago an entertainer named Dan Emmett was leaving the theater when he was hailed by its manager, "Dan, we need a new song right away. Can you come up with something that'll put excitement into the show? We need your talents desperately."

The next day was a rainy one, so Dan Emmett stayed home to think over the request. As he walked about the room the phrase, "I wish I was in Dixie" ran repeatedly through his mind. With that good start, his inspired pen soon had a complete song down on paper. "Dixie" was a smash hit the moment it was published. People have been light-heartedly singing and whistling it ever since.

All because of a simple request.

Incidentally, mature and self-reliant individuals often tend to forget and ignore this system for winning their way. They somehow have the feeling their independence demands that they do everything for themselves, but the fact is, this is an interdependent world where we all need each other. It is a sign of neither selfishness nor weakness to ask things from other people; when properly done, it is the mark of an intelligent person.

To keep his staff of salesmen reminded of the value of the simple request, one sales manager has printed this stirring message on the wall of the conference room:

Ask all!

Ask all you meet.

Ask all the time.

Ask all the ways.

Ask all over again.

Ask all!

While we are still on the subject of making known your requests, let's add this good plan: *Don't hesitate to ask more of people.*

A man once told me, somewhat proudly, "You know, I get everything I ask from people."

I told him, "Then you are not asking for nearly enough. And the reason you don't ask for more is because you are afraid you won't get it. Anyone can get a little if he asks for a little. It takes genuine courage to ask for something when there is some doubt in your mind whether or not you will get it. Keep asking without any regard as to whether or not you will get it. If you have the courage to stick with it, you will eventually get much more."

The test is simple enough. Draw up a two-column list. In the left-hand space write down what you want from people. In the right-hand column write down what you are getting. How do they compare? Maybe the reason you are not getting more is because you are not tactfully asking for more. It is just as much your right to ask things of other people as it is for them to ask of you; so no longer hesitate. That is how you may find your two columns balancing to your total satisfaction.

You can get others to promote your interests once you learn:

How to Predict What People Will Do

Every once in a while you watch a television drama in which you see a certain type of interesting action. It is often climactic to the plot and usually goes something like this:

Our Western hero is sent as an ambassador of peace by the U. S. Army to a warlike tribe of Indians. As evening falls he rides alone and fearlessly into the Indian camp, followed and surrounded by warriors in fierce warpaint. Our hero takes his place around the campfire and tries to talk the stern-faced chief and his medicine man out of their warlike intentions. He politely warns them that the white men have mighty weapons capable of destroying the entire tribe with one fiery blast.

The chief, really being a good sort of Indian at heart, is inclined to talk peace with our hero. But not the medicine man. He dances in rage around the campfire, shaking his spear at the darkening sky.

Just as the medicine man is about to win the growling braves over to the side of war, our hero slowly and with great deliberation rises to his feet. With folded arms he looks up at the full moon hanging motionless in the clear evening sky. Our hero's silent and mysterious manner causes a hush to fall on the tribe. Wonderingly, all stare upward at the moon. Our hero speaks with authority: "To prove the mighty power of the white man ... I command the moon to disappear!"

Our hero raises his hand skyward. A gasp escapes the tribe as darkness slowly creeps across the face of the moon. As the moon disappears the Indians fall to their knees in trembling awe.

A moment later our hero again raises his hand—and the shadow crawls off the moon, leaving it full and bright and yellow. The medicine man drops his spear and creeps away. The warriors gaze in admiration at our hero. The chief embraces him as a brother. Peace has been won.

Because our hero knew something about the science of astronomy he could accurately predict that eclipse of the moon. That gave him the power to persuade the tribe toward peace.

Likewise if you can predict how a man will react in a particular situation, you can employ your prediction for winning your way.

How can you build your persuasiveness through your powers of prophecy? That is what we want to find out right now.

The first vital principle to remember when predicting human behavior is that we human beings do not always act as logically or as beneficially as we like to think we do. That is why you must not expect others to act the way you think they *should* act. Human beings are often illogical, fickle, evasive. You cannot walk up to a man and ask him how he will react to a certain situation, for his reply will be slanted perhaps by a desire to appear very wise, or it may be colored by his attempt to live up to his self-image of being a courageous individual. He will tell you what he wants you to believe about himself, plus what he wants to believe about himself.

In his book *Why People Buy,* Louis Cheskin further explains:

People's behavior is not predictable by asking them what they will do or how they will act in relation to a product. They either don't know what they will do or they think they know but don't think they should tell you.[19]

So if people do not always respond to your persuasions according to clear-thinking logic, what *does* motivate them to vote for this political candidate or to buy that make of automobile or to go along with this man's ideas? Let's find out.

People react according to their *dominating desires* and to their habitual emotional states. The stronger the desire the more forceful the reaction. If you offer self-advancement to any man you can be sure of an eagerly agreeable response; everyone wants to get ahead. If you propose a daring plan of action to a timid person you can accurately predict hesitation and indecision on his part. By studying the inner man of the other man you can discover what *really* motivates him. From there you can prophecy his behavior with an astonishing degree of success.

> The story is recalled about the lawyer who called one afternoon at a luxurious country estate to transact some legal business with a wealthy client. As he entered he saw that tea was being served to a number of guests, several attractive women among them. The dignified hostess approached and handed him a cup of tea with the invitation, "If you like, there are some nice cookies in the next room." The lawyer declined with, "No thanks, I already have a date with a blonde."

That is a humorous illustration of how a man responds according to his private interests, according to what he really has on his mind. Had that hostess understood him a bit better, she would not have offered him pastry-type cookies!

Let's examine two more dominating desires which make people respond as they do:

---

19 *Why People Buy,* by Louis Chesldin.   By permission of LIVERIGHT, Publishers, N. Y. Copyright 1959, by Louis Cheskin.

1. People desire to impress others with their better qualities, while minimizing or hiding the less acceptable ones. This is an oh-so-obvious trait of human nature, nevertheless one that should be remembered when you want to establish harmonious interpersonal relations. Everyone likes to appear in the best light possible; *however,* our inner responses to a situation will be according to how we *really* feel toward it. It is important that you learn the secret thoughts and feelings of the other man.

    Example:

    I once heard the supervisor of a chain gasoline station give a talk to a group of new employees. What he said to them indicated expert ability to predict the reactions of motorists who drove in. He told them, "Whenever a man tells you to fill up his tank, don't overfill it to where you spill gas on the ground. He may not say anything to you about it because he doesn't want to appear cheap, but you can be sure that he's feeling resentment of some sort. After all, you are wasting his gasoline."

2. A doctor who makes frequent lecture tours around this city once had this to say during a newspaper interview:

    I have five different talks dealing with various matters of healthy and happy living. I can always predict which meetings will draw the largest audience. It will be the one where I announce my subject as sex.

Of course. Any healthy individual will respond with aroused interest in anything relating to sex. This is nothing new to the professional persuaders. They predict quite accurately a heavy purchase of those vitamins and soaps and styles which promise to make a man more manly and to turn a lady into a slyly seductive sorceress- Happily for all this, both sexes eagerly go along with the persuasive promises.

Nature sees to it that women do their best to look good to men. And in all recorded history there has never been a single case of any sensible healthy male who preferred playing checkers to making love.

Summary: Self-knowledge is the greatest power you possess for predicting another's behavior or for understanding his desires. How does self-information supply you with facts about the other person? Like this: If you clearly see your own desires and motives and passions you will be able to discern them in others. For one thing, insight into your own nature enables you to reflect, "Well, this is how I would respond in this particular situation, therefore, the other person would also respond according to the same laws governing human behavior." Let someone hold up before you a dish of delicious strawberry shortcake topped with whipped cream and a merry cherry. You will respond with desire to consume it. Do you think the person next to you feels any differently? Not if he's human!

Easy Ways to Win Promotion

1. Keep adding valuable people to your life. Make yourself valuable to them.

2. Whatever your plans may be, get as much help as possible from other people. Interdependence is a cheery law of life.

3. Follow the eight rules given in this chapter for investing in rich contacts.

4. Remember the story of Brigadier General John J. Pershing. Let it keep you excited at your own opportunities for promotion.

5. Decide that you will establish the types of atmospheres that contribute most to your plans.

6. Never permit a negative atmosphere to turn you into its own kind, rather switch it into the positive kind you want.

7. Freely permit others to contribute to your advancement. They need to feel needed.

8. Develop the art of simply asking for what you want. Use the various techniques offered throughout this book.

9. You probably should ask for more from people. The reason so many people have so little is because they ask for so little.

10. You can predict human behavior to an amazingly accurate degree. Use this power for getting others to promote your interests.

10

PERSONAL POWERS THAT MAKE YOU A LEADER AND AN AUTHORITY

Have you ever noticed the tremendous attraction that *power* has for all of us? Power of all kinds hypnotizes our attention and excites our emotions: The giant space rocket sends a thrill through us as it zooms powerfully skyward. Crashing thunder and leaping lightning hold us in a strange sort of fascination. Notice how the grand mightiness of music causes us to hold our breath, as when hearing the throbbing rhythm of *The Battle Hymn of the Republic.*

Wherever you find it, "Power, like the diamond, dazzles the beholder." (Colton)

That is why we now want to dig into the topic of *personal power. Your* power. This is the element that not only makes you as dazzling as you need to be, but it is the blazing torch that lights your path toward leadership and authority.

Whether you realize it or not, *your need for power is already matched by your possession of that energy.* Accept this as a fact. Your acceptance makes possible your personal forcefulness. Niagara Falls is powerful, but man had to first of all realize and accept its power as already existing.

That turned its power into creativity. States Dr. Rollo May, ". . . the unique powers and initiative of each individual must be rediscovered, and used as a basis for work which contributes to the good . . ."[20]

The goal of this chapter is to turn what you really *are* into what you can really *do*. Power-packed action will be your daily experience.

A survey made by a group of psychologists at one of our universities came up with the conclusion that individual strength was the most admired character trait of all. This is easy to understand, inasmuch as character-strength is made up of so many praiseworthy traits, such as maturity, decisiveness, courtesy, and the ability to think independently.

One of the friendliest facts you will ever encounter is that personal power can lead you to everything you want from others. People gladly associate with and give to the strong person. Why? Because he gives *them* both the sense of security and the gentle guidance that they need. We like to be around the man who is sure of himself because he makes us a bit surer of ourselves. Think about those people to whom you are especially attracted and you will find that they possess above-average portions of individual strength. Sir Winston Churchill is a perfect historical example of a man whose private power burst forth into public prominence and acclaim.

The wise American author Walt Whitman once penned, "Nothing endures but personal qualities."

We can accurately add, "Nothing works quite so well in human relations as personal qualities." Sometimes after looking around for all sorts of guides and helps for living a more powerful life we make a complete circle and come right back to those standard virtues which we were taught in childhood. Somehow, every man realizes that when all is said and done it takes the old-fashioned virtue of courage to build an effective life, and that it requires the quality of patience to see us through a temporary setback, and that there is nothing like plain old persistence for winning our way through the world of people. Deep

---

20 Rollo May, Ph.D., *Mans Search for Himself* (New York: W. W. Norton and Company, Inc., 1953).

within himself every man knows that these are the essentials which always have worked for him and which always will work in his behalf.

Not only does private power supply you with public leadership and authority, but it contributes in a very special manner to your daily enjoyment of life. Henry Wadsworth Longfellow declares, "To be strong is to be happy."

With all these benefits in mind, let's identify five of your major strengths, then go on to discover how they can add to your influence over people. They are:

1. Self-Resourcefulness

2. Self-Determination

3. Self-Influence

4. Self-Insight

5. Self-Correction

The first point we want to make is that you release your dynamic energies for leadership and authority when you:

Employ Your Self-Resourcefulness

Some students of the Civil War believe that Nathan Bedford Forrest was the foxiest general to appear in that conflict. Why do they rank him alongside or even above such notable commanders as Robert E. Lee, Stonewall Jackson, U.S. Grant? Because General Forrest had fully developed that high-powered character trait which we call *Self-Resourcefulness.*

> Legend has it that one afternoon Forrest was leading 50 of his Confederate troopers on a raid of the countryside. Suddenly, as they rounded a turn in the road, there appeared before them 1,000 Union soldiers. It was hard to say which side was more shocked by the trap which the Confederates had run into—but it was Forrest who instantly called upon his inner originalities.

He yelled loudly while pointing excitedly toward the sky, at the same time signaling to his men that they should imitate his action, which they promptly did. While the Union soldiers stared puzzled at whatever they were supposed to see in the blue sky, Forrest and his troops galloped to safety.

You are 10 times more resourceful than you think you are.

Because you are, you can achieve 10 times as much as you think you can.

"I don't know about that," commented Phillip E., who had an air of defeat and discouragement about him. "I just can't seem to reach inside myself and withdraw anything useful."

"Where," I asked, "do you need to be self-resourceful?"

"Quite frankly, in getting along with the little lady in my life. I'd like a little less fussing between us and a little more fun. Is that asking too much?"

"What have you done about it?"

"Nothing that really works. I'm confused."

"Then the first resourceful thing you can do is to clarify your thinking toward the problem. A confused mind can produce only confused and worthless actions—as you already know."

He nodded painfully. "How well I know."

"Why don't you handle the problem with some originality?"

"Make a suggestion."

"Stop fighting the situation and try to understand what is involved in it. Haven't you noticed that the more you fight a problem the worse it gets?"

"Yes. Why is that?"

"Because you are trying to win an argument instead of solving the problem. An argument can never be won, it can only be harmful. Learn to place your personal interests ahead of your angry pride. Don't defend your vanity, go after a pleasant relationship. You can continue to sacrifice yourself to your pride if you want, but don't complain when you lose out on what you could have had."

Phillip was thoughtful for a moment, then said, "You suggested that I should stop fighting the problem. All right. I'm willing. Please tell me exactly what to do."

"Employ the technique of *Reverse Reaction*. This means that whenever you and your lady approach a crisis in your relationship, you react in reverse of any negativities she may display. If she's angry, you stay sweet. If she criticizes you, fail to criticize in return. If she angrily withdraws from you, do not also withdraw from her."

"It sounds so simple."

"That is exactly why you haven't used it. Your prides and your confusions and your hurts have unnecessarily complicated things."

"Reverse Reaction. Sounds interesting. What will happen when I use it?"

"Why don't you find out for yourself?"

Phillip did. It worked. It had to work. Once he refused to struggle with the problem it ceased to be one. Phillip's lady discovered that he was really a much nicer man than she had thought. Phillip also discovered that his lady was far more pleasant than he had given her credit for.

The tremendous principle of Reverse Reaction never fails. It is a perfect resource which gives you quiet mastery over people and circumstances.

Try it. See for yourself.

The Miracle of Self-Determination

You have your choice of living your own life or of letting other people live it for you. The more you live your own, the greater personal power you will have with other people; the less you determine your own activities the less influence you have. It is really as simple as that.

"The question is," a prominent clergyman remarked in a recent television appearance, "how much of your life is determined by *your* choices."

You can, if you choose, let other people run your life for you. And I guarantee that in the long run they will contribute more to its ruin than to its construction.

Don't waste your time and energies wondering about the opinions of others toward you. Learn to ignore criticism. Take it as a compliment that they need you to criticize, and keep plunging ahead. Never permit another person to determine your decisions or your beliefs or your emotional moods. Your feelings not only belong to you, but you are in masterful control of them, that is, if you will only *take* the control that is really yours.

When you make responses to other people, make up your mind that you will respond as you really want to, not according to what is expected of you. Above all, never react in a certain way just because you have been doing it that way for years. Don't be afraid to walk into a room full of people without a customary smile on your face. At first people will think that you are worried about something because they themselves do not smile when they are worried. But after a while they will see that the reason you do not smile as much as they do is because you have dissolved the need to give the impression of being unworried. They will be attracted to you because you are more real than they are.

An American who exerted profound influence on millions of his fellow citizens and who today is regarded as one of the most powerful thinkers ever produced in this country once wrote as follows: "What I must do is all that concerns me, not what the people think. This rule . . . may serve for the whole distinction between greatness and meanness. It is the harder, because you will always find those who think they know what is your duty better than you know it ... the great man is he who in the midst of the crowd keeps with perfect sweetness the independence of solitude."

It was such individualism that made Ralph Waldo Emerson the power-for-good that he was.

Also, Self-Determination is the cause of more financial success in the world than can be imagined. For instance:

There was once a man who during his lifetime was able to give more than $350,000,000 to worthy causes. One of the reasons he amassed so much wealth was because he had made up his mind that he and Self-Determination were going to march together up the road to financial fortune. An incident that occurred when he was a minor official of a Pennsylvania railroad will show how this power served to make him an outstanding employee. One day an accident occurred which blocked the normal rail traffic. Only one man could give the official order which would clear the tracks and get traffic back to its normal flow. That man was Superintendent Thomas A. Scott. The minor official went in search of Scott, but he couldn't be found. The traffic continued to line up on both sides of the wreck. The situation grew desperate. That minor official decided that someone had to have the courage to make a decision, so he made it on the spot by giving the order to clear the tracks. The engines and cars were soon rolling forward again. When Superintendent Scott heard that his employee had taken personal charge of the situation he commended him for his individualism and topped the commendation with a raise in salary.

That is how Self-Determination carried that railroad official all the way to the top in the world of industry and finance. His name was Andrew Carnegie.

You can clear your path toward Self-Determination by re-membering that:

Self-Influence Is the Greatest Influence There Is

We used to have a shaggy collie dog who had grown somewhat careless in his thinking habits. Whenever the hounds down the street started barking, our collie lazily lifted his head, stared straight ahead with boredom, and yelped unenthusiastically a few times. He didn't really know why he was doing what he was doing; it was much as if he shrugged the thought, "The others are barking; guess I'm supposed to bark too."

We need not fall into a thinking-trap like Fido. None of us need to sway before the pointless influence of other people, much less do what they do because it seems to be the proper thing to do. Unfortunately, lots of people do.

If you are not alert, even such an impersonal element as the weather can cover you with a negative influence. Tests made recently by a group of psychologists show that people are less happy and more irritable during gloomy weather. Why? Because they carelessly permit clouds and cold winds to seep into their systems, thus making them as gloomy on the inside as the weather is on the outside. If something like this ever happens to you, resist being influenced and victimized by fully realizing that you are permitting an impersonal element to personally affect you.

Self-Influence is the greatest kind of influence there is!

That is why you should make up your mind right now that *you* are going to be influenced by *you*.

Harold J., a junior executive, made up his mind that he was go-ing to do just that. As he dropped into my office, he said, "I feel that I could get places a lot faster by tackling this problem of outside influence."

"I asked, "What's the specific problem?"

He replied, "I'm not sure, except that I don't know how to influence myself with my own sound judgments and ideas. I believe they are just as good as the next man's, but still, I give in too easily to others—and more often than not, they are wrong. I don't mind making my own mistakes, but who wants to follow the other man into a snare? I'm tired of drifting on the currents of the other man's mind. How can I straighten myself out?"

"You already suggested the solution. Influence yourself toward thinking for yourself."

"How do I do that?"

"Down at the office, whenever someone suggests a course of action, stop right there and say to yourself, 'All right, that's what he thinks should be done, but what do I think? Honestly, now, what do I think?' Draw yourself as close as possible to what you *really* think and feel about it. If your ideas turn out contrary to his, quietly suggest them to him. He is not afraid to tell you what *he* thinks, so why should you hesitate toward him? Practice this technique during the next few weeks."

Harold nodded. "I can see how that would place me under my own influence. All right. I'll make it a habit to ask myself, 'Honestly, Harold, what do *you* think?'"

"Fine. That question has a way of drawing your own good judgments out of the pool of mere public opinion. You will eventually find yourself capable of ten times your present independence. Actually, you are far sharper than you think. This is the way to prove it."

It's a delightful day when a man discovers for himself that Self-Influence is the best kind of influence there is. "Doubt whom you will, but never yourself." (Bovee)

Develop Your Power of Self-Insight

A sure road toward understanding the other man—and thereby influencing him—is to first understand yourself. "He who knows himself knows others." (Colton) Self-Insight is one of the richest treasures you possess, and one which is never exhausted; you can always discover more value within yourself. By Self-Insight we mean the ability to understand why we act as we do and why we think along certain lines. It means examining our opinions and convictions to discover why we have them in the first place and why we cling to them so passionately.

To develop adequate Self-Insight we must frankly face ourselves as we actually are, not as we would like to see ourselves or as we want others to see us.

How does this relate to your power to master and command people? Well, remember that human behavior follows certain basic patterns. Therefore, if you can get first-hand knowledge of its principles by observing yourself in action, you enable yourself to predict the attitudes and behavior of the other man. You already do this to some extent or other. For instance, you enter a friend's backyard and find him adding the finishing touches to his homemade barbecue pit. You know very well that he wouldn't at all mind a compliment or two on his skill in building the pit. How do you know what he wants and needs from you? Because you yourself wouldn't at all mind a word of praise in a similar situation. Your insight into your own need for a kind word enables you to understand his need, therefore you say the thing that influences him toward you in a favorable way. That is a very obvious example of the persuasive force found in self-knowledge. Its development can empower you far more than may be obvious to you at present.

Listen to what Professor Ernest R. Groves has to say:

He who is sound in his knowledge of himself is most likely to meet successfully the social problems that confront him in life. His willingness to scrutinize himself shows a fact-facing disposition which augurs well for any undertaking. More than this, it indicates his thorough-going determination to discover the resources he has at hand . . .[21]

A New Yorker who runs a travel agency uses his Self-Insight to earn more money. His system is really as simple as it is profitable.

He asks himself, "If I came into my agency as a prospective traveler, what would I want the owner to say to me? How could he appeal most effectively to me?" He then makes a list of phrases which would persuade *himself* to buy a ticket, such as:

"You'll meet new friends."

'It's an exciting adventure."

"You'll get away from it all."

"Travel keeps you youthful."

"You'll be surprised at all your fun."

These key phrases form a part of his talks with prospective clients, and are included in his advertising material. They never fail to hit home, for they hit the prospect squarely in his desire for something different and something more adventurous.

Earlier in this book we spoke of the need to become aware of what you want from your interpersonal relations. Now you have still another reason for acquiring this awareness. That reason is this: You must have an idea of what you want if you are to understand what other people want, for your basic needs are the very same as those longed for by others. By knowing what they need you can satisfy them; by satisfying them you can influence them.

---

21 *Understanding Yourself,* by Ernest R. Groves, Rev. Ed. 1949; copyright 1939, 1941 by Emerson Books, Inc. Reprinted by permission of the publishers.

Ask yourself how well you know yourself. To that very same degree you will know and control others.

Self-Insight is a personal power you should start developing to maximum use right now. I have never known a man who had it who didn't also have the magic power to persuade and command people.

The Profit of Self-Correction

Recently at a dinner in Hollywood an executive in the entertainment business was telling me of a major problem of his. He explained, "It's the attitudes of some of the people whom I try to help get ahead. It's strange how reluctant they are to admit to making a mistake or to concede that something has them baffled. They are of the opinion that I'll think less of them unless they are 100 percent efficient. Little do they know how much I admire the man who admits his shortcomings. That's the man I can help—and the man who can help himself to an advanced career."

There is something humanly likeable about admitting one's shortcomings and errors. And there is something extra appealing about the person who faces his need for correction. It takes mature strength to admit and solve problems in our business practices and within the home circle. One of the best things about Self-Correction is this: If we do it, others won't be so tempted to try and do it for us! We retain our independence.

People generally take one of two courses when confronted by a problem needing correction. One course, unfortunately chosen too frequently, is to get involved with the emotional factors surrounding the situation. When this happens a person loses his ability to think clearly and to act accurately, and as a consequence is unable to serve his own best interests. Any of the negative emotions, such as envy and self-pity, are bound to swell both the problem and the pressure on the person involved with it.

The other choice—and the courageous one—is to stubbornly set your mind on the problem itself. It is amazing how quickly we can clear things up simply by giving our earnest and wholehearted attention to the very thing which bothers us.

One of the wisest actions you can ever take is to develop a *Correction Consciousness.* This simply means that you build within yourself an *enthusiastic desire to correct your problems,* and not to fight them or evade them or weep over them. It means that your only objective is a satisfying solution. Nothing else counts; nothing else will be tolerated.

Here are three sound suggestions for building your all-important Correction Consciousness:

1. Recently a woman dropped me a friendly note thanking me for help she had received from a previous book of mine.[22] She wrote:

    Dear Mr. Howard:

    I've just learned something about daily achievement. Something exciting! That exciting thing is that there is always a right way to do anything! All a person really needs to do is find that right way. That guarantees his success. If we fail to get what we want it is only because we have not grasped that simple but spectacular truth.

    People are funny. They brood over the wrong way, instead of thinking in terms of correction. Just because they don't see the proper procedure they foolishly believe it doesn't exist. Believe me, the answer is always there. I know. I personally prove it every day.

    The best reason for believing in the existence of a right solution to your problem is that it really exists.

---

22 Vernon Howard, *Success Through the Magic of Personal Power* (Englewood Cliffs, N. J.: Prentice-Hall, Inc., 1961).

2. Continually ask yourself, "Which do I want most-progress or retreat?" The very asking of the question has a way of nudging you toward Self-Correction. Once you realize that you can either go forward or be left behind, you are quite naturally going to take the course that serves your best interests.

An acquaintance of mine was once told by his employer that he was out of place working at an office desk which required so much accuracy with bookkeeping duties. For the moment the employee was stunned and hurt, but immediately started looking around for a solution. Going to the personnel office he requested a transfer to the public relations department. Because he made up his mind to correct the problem he eventually corrected himself all the way to his private office with his name on the door.

3. A British patrol in India was once pursued by enemy troops. The commanding officer ordered his patrol to retreat into the mouth of a nearby valley. He at once saw his mistake, for the opposite end of the valley was blocked by an impassable mountain peak. The officer acted at once. He swung his patrol around, and before the pursuers had time to trap them, the soldiers dashed out of the valley to freedom.

Remember that one of the greatest principles for human growth and personal enrichment is: *never try to protect a mistake*. The more we attempt to justify a false position the more we are bound by it. Whenever you make an error, look at it squarely-even cheerfully—and then take immediate action. Don't wait for the ideal solution to pop up; it never does. Just go ahead with whatever imperfect plans seem best for the time. This is the honest and courageous Self-Correction that carries your human relations from fair to good to superb in the shortest time possible.

Power-Builders From This Chapter

1. Psychologists, philosophers, and wise men of all ages agree whole-heartedly that every man possesses 10 times the power he actually uses. Make it your aim to prove it to yourself.

2. Personal power is the single greatest attraction you have. When fully released, it charms people and lures fortune.

3. Remember the value of the five self-powers covered in this chapter. "All who become men of power reach their estate by self-mastery." (J. G. Holland)

4. Practice the technique of Reverse Reaction. Don't be surprised when it serves you with unexpected authority.

5. Make up your mind that *you* are going to live *your* life. There is no one on earth with a better right to it.

6. Do you want good measures of leadership and authority? If so, start influencing yourself with the idea that they *can* be won. Once you are convinced that you can have them, you will! We commonly call this the power of faith.

7. Social skill is largely a result of knowing that person whom you call *you*. Get better acquainted with your self.

8. Cultivate a Correction Consciousness.

9. Never forget that there is always a successful way to do anything you really want to do.

10. Every time you correct yourself you charge yourself with extra personal strength. Make enough corrections and you will have more than enough people who will want to do things for you. If you don't believe it, try it.

YOUR PERSONALITY CAN MAKE YOU POWERFULLY PERSUASIVE

A man doesn't fail in life because he has certain weaknesses; he fails because he doesn't possess certain strengths.

One of those major strengths which guarantee a man's fortunes is a persuasive personality. That is the magical magnet that effortlessly draws to a man his social success and his financial prosperity and everything else he desires from life. As a typical illustration, a recent newspaper story told of a salesman who called for the first time upon the chief executive of a large department store. So impressed was the executive by the salesman's attractive personality that he not only placed a large order for the salesman's products but offered his visitor a topnotch position with the store.

There exist a surprising number of false notions concerning human personality. One of the most damaging of these mistaken attitudes is that a person is hopelessly stuck with whatever mediocrity he happens to find himself with. That is nothing but a myth, and one which we will expose in this chapter.

Typical of another attitude which needs drastic revision was the one expressed by a woman who told me:

"I would like nothing better than to have a more attractive and more poised personality, but I don't seem to possess the inner resources. If I could only believe that I have something worth developing I know I could go on from there to success of some sort. But I feel so inwardly empty, so powerless."

I asked her, "Haven't you noticed the dozens of urges you have?"

"Like what?"

"Like wanting to speak up at a meeting, rather than remaining silent. Like the desire to become a nicer person. Like coming right out and telling yourself what you really want out of life."

She laughed, "Don't forget my urge to kick off my tight shoes—company or no company."

"Notice these urges. They are evidences of your other self wanting to break through. For one reason or another you have hidden them. But these constant desires to do something *different* indicate that you do have inner resources of personality-power. All they need is release. You are the one who can release them."

Everyone possesses inner urges which can be released in the service of a brighter self. Later in this chapter you will be shown a way to *free* your forceful personality.

There is really nothing mysterious about it. When you come right down to the facts, personality is nothing more or less than the way you habitually think and act toward others. Act pleasantly and people will credit you with a pleasant personality; move with energy and enthusiasm and others will think of you as a lively individual; think with decisiveness and self-command and people are certain to respect you as a person of considerable strength. Your personality consists of what you do and what you don't do, in what you say and how you say it, in your over-all manner when you are with others.

How important is a winning personality? Here is the supreme value placed upon it by Professor H. A. Overstreet:

As individuals, our chief task in life is to make our personality, and what our personality has to offer, effective in our particular environment of human beings.[23]

The Commander and the Commanded

There are two types of personalities in the world:

There is the *Commander.*
And there is the *Commanded.*

The Commander is the type who has no trouble influencing people and conditions to his liking. Not only that but his personality is in constant demand. People constantly seek him out. There just aren't enough of his kind to go around. People need the leader who can show them what to do and how to do it and make them like it better and better. Benjamin Franklin and Thomas Jefferson are fine historical examples of the Commander type of personality.

What about the Commanded individual? One thing about him is certain: His people-persuading powers hover around the zero mark. Moreover, to his special distress, he has but slight influence over himself. The words and acts and attitudes of other people push him this way and that. As you can imagine, he is not exactly bombarded by success of any kind.

You can choose to be either kind of personality.

You can be the Commander.

Or you can be the Commanded.

I don't think you will hesitate between those choices.

No one is completely one or the other. Most people hit a balancing blend of both types of personalities. However, the aim of this chapter is to multiply those superior powers of which you are actually capable.

---

23 H. A. Overstreet, *Influencing Human Behavior* (New York: W. W. Norton and Company, Inc., 1925).

In order to do this, we are first going to look at extreme examples of both kinds of personalities. We need to see how they act; also, we will benefit by gaining insight into their attitudes and their emotional patterns. Our knowledge of them serves as a window through which we can see just what we must do and what we must avoid doing.

As you read these traits and attitudes you may find yourself responding to some of them. You might reflect, "Yes, that's the way I sometimes feel." This is a good thing, for it means that you are storing up self-knowledge.   Any truth which you discover about your personality — favorable or unfavorable — is a truth that sets you free from negativity.

First let's look at a person who is pretty much in the camp of the Commanded:

He personalizes things too much, hence his feelings are hurt at the slightest hint of criticism or disapproval.

he is always doing things he really doesn't want to do, just so people will like him.

Our man is considerably confused; he never quite knows what to do next.

he wrongly concludes that it is his intelligence which is at fault, when in truth it is his inhibited personality.

He wonders what people think of him and usually concludes the worst.

our man is much too serious. he mistakenly thinks that seriousness is the same thing as earnestness, which it isn't.

He thinks that happy people are too shallow to realize how grim and troublesome life actually is.

he is forever waiting for something to come from the outside to make him feel good on the inside.

Whenever he feels like doing something adventurous, he first has to find out whether someone else did it without getting hurt.

he doesn't like himself too well but he honestly doesn't know what to do about it.

It is other people who determine his emotions. Their action automatically triggers his reaction of joy or depression or whatever. He doesn't realize that he can actually determine the kind of feelings he wants to feel.

he often believes that he gives more than he gets and secretly resents it.

He is hounded by his fears and mistakenly believes that there is no other way to live.

the commanded man is continually surprised to find that his plans for self-advancement seldom work. he had such high hopes — again.

He is a slave to the unfavorable influences of other people and is bound by unhappy circumstances and is snarled by his very own negative thinking habits.

Happily, there is no need whatsoever for him to remain in his inferior condition. Every Commanded personality has the inner abilities to turn himself into a Commander.

Now let's see what goes on in the life of the commanding type of personality:

Whenever he wants something, he goes directly after it, and never minds who says he can't or shouldn't.

he doesn't have to fight to control resentment and hostility; he is pretty much free of them.

He may occasionally feel a bit timid about doing something adventurous for the first time, but that is the very last thing that prevents him from going ahead anyway.

the commander possesses tremendous energy because he never permits people or circumstances to drain him.

He takes immediate charge of circumstances, whatever they might be, and turns them into what he wants them to be.

people like to be around him because they recognize and admire his inner strength.

He knows that no one can insult him or hurt him without his permission. He never grants it.

the spontaneity and unexpectedness of his personality delight everyone.

He is able to like people fully and freely, for the simple reason that there is no psychological confusion in him that makes it necessary for him to dislike people.

because he is his naturally unpretentious self, he never has to worry about getting found out.

When he asks others to do something, they do it willingly and happily. His winning personality makes others want to go along with him.

he has little hesitation in doing what he really wants to do and even less hesitation in not doing what he really does not want to do.

He knows that life can be taken seriously, but that that need not mean taking it gloomily or sourly or unhappily.

the commander is too busily attracting favorable responses from people to wonder much about what they think of him.

Robert Louis Stevenson, beloved author of *Treasure Island*, possessed the personality of a Commander. His biographers agree that he was not only a literary genius but a wholly charming gentleman and friend. Stevenson had that magic touch which turned all whom he met into admirers, men and women alike. His philosophy for self-improvement might be summed up like this:

"Never be satisfied by your performances, yet never be cast down by them. Just educate yourself continually as you go along. Results will take care of themselves in a delightfully surprising way."

You couldn't find a simpler philosophy for growing more attractive. No one who really practiced it could ever fail to present a more appealing personality.

How to Release Your Personality Power

A bright and persuasive personality emerges when a man frees himself from his false self. This false self consists of timidities and inhibitions which were picked up somewhere along the road. It is made up of ideas and attitudes and beliefs that have never worked and never will. The false self is *acquired*; we never had it as children, and that is why young folks are far more emotionally honest than adults and also why you don't have to give sleeping pills to your son or daughter. Society has not yet taught them to deceive themselves about what they want from life, therefore, they are not in night-time conflict between the real and the false selves.

Underneath a man's acquired personality is the real person who is rich in happiness and forceful in natural influence. This is not some psychological theory or merely a comforting thought; it is a fact which any earnest individual can discover for himself. Here is what Dr. Harry Emerson Fosdick has to say about it: "We possess by nature the factors out of which personality can be made, and to organize them into effective personal life is every man's primary responsibility."[24]

---

24 Harry Emerson Fosdick, *On Being a Real Person* (New York: Harper and Brothers, 1943).

You can develop your genuine and far-more-attractive personality by steadily disengaging yourself from mistaken notions toward life and people.

There is no principle of life more simple nor more accurate than this: If you do the right things you will get right results. Now, there is a variation of that rule which is just as effective but frequently overlooked by those in search of personal freedom. That variation is: If you will stop doing the wrong things you will stop getting wrong results. Listed below you find some of those acts and attitudes that should be disengaged from a man's life. Free yourself from them and your personality-power surges forward abundantly:

1. Never hesitate to shed unprofitable programs.

2. Don't think it is up to you to save the world.

3. Permit no one to tell you what you want from life.

4. Don't condemn yourself for being you.

5. Don't feel guilty over a loved one's mistakes.

6. Never agree to an unfair relationship.

7. Don't let domineering people bluff you.

8. Don't joke with people who won't get the point.

9. Never hesitate to employ new methods of persuasion.

10. Don't believe anyone has power to trap you.

11. Ignore advice given by confused friends.

12. Don't believe that gentleness is weakness.

13. Don't give in to excessive demands upon your energy.

14. Don't pre-plan your social acts and attitudes.

15. Don't be afraid to love the lovable.

16. Never hesitate to declare your purposes to yourself.

17. Don't think you have to explain yourself to others.

18. Never believe that circumstances are unchangeable.

19. Don't allow another's distress to upset you.

20. Don't underestimate your ability to sway others.

Let's go into detail with point 14: Don't pre-plan your social acts and attitudes.

Carefully watch yourself the next time you enter a room filled with people. If you are earnestly observant you will find yourself hurriedly reviewing just what you will say and how you will act. We all do this to some extent or other, though we are rarely aware of it. We even adopt the facial expression which we think suitable for the occasion. We do this of course because we quite naturally want to make the best possible impression.

The trouble with these pre-planned attitudes is that they rob our personalities of their ability to do the unexpected or the delightful thing that attracts people to us. It is the suddenly surprising person who catches our interest. Have you noticed that you can just about predict what some people are going to say and do? Also notice that while such folks may be perfectly pleasant, they are also somewhat dull.

Make this experiment: The next several times you meet people, *enter the relationship with no pre-planned ideas of how you should act.* Empty your mind of all urges to say a certain thing or to act out a particular mannerism. Make no predeterminations of any kind of impression to make. Enter the room as if you don't give a hoot whether or not you make a good impression. Be careless. Be indifferent. "One must learn to drop inhibitions, self-consciousness ... and dignity."[25]

------

25 A. H. Maslow, *Motivation and Personality* (New York: Harper and Brothers, 1954).

What will happen? For one thing you need not fear that you will say the wrong thing. Your resourceful mind is much too sharp for that. It will think of something, and *if left to its own originalities you will come up with something far more clever or kindly or surprising or persuasive than you ever thought possible.* You will experience genuine self-expression. Your true personality will be in action.

This exercise frees your personality from those old and repetitious actions which block spontaneity. Have you ever thought of just the right thing to say — but only when it was too late to do so? Well, this technique enables you to say just the right thing at just the right time! As an example, I was recently standing with a group of people when a husband approached and slipped his arm around his wife's waist. Someone grinningly remarked to him, "You seem to like what you've found." The husband's enthusiastic and wholly charming reply was, "Yes, and if no one claims her in thirty days I get to keep her!"

Don't pre-plan your acts and attitudes. If you will practice this method, really practice, you will see delightful things happening to your personality. It works. It works for you. Work with it.

Make Yourself Comfortable

You probably remember reading the classic story entitled *Gulliver's Travels.* This exciting and imaginative book was penned back in 1726 by Jonathan Swift, considered one of the most brilliant authors ever to write in the English language.

Here is how the plot unfolds:

Gulliver sets sail from England with his destination as the South Seas. A furious storm strikes the ship, driving it off course and into strange waters. The violent winds pick up Gulliver and toss him into the churning sea. While floundering around he sights a mysterious little island in the distance. Using all his strength he manages to swim to shore.

While stretched out and sleeping in exhaustion he is discovered by the little people of the island—the island of Lilliput. Because the Lilliputians are no larger than Gulliver's thumb, they are alarmed at the size and power of the sleeping giant. They swiftly bind him with ropes and stakes. With the aid of 1500 tiny horses—each about four and one-half inches high— they manage to drag their gigantic prisoner to the city where the Emperor of Lilliput awaits.

What is to be done with this Living Mountain? That is the perplexing question faced by the anxious Lilliputians. Unchain him and he might angrily destroy them. Even to permit him to walk around might be dangerous; a few careless steps would crush their homes and orchards.

In other words, the tiny people feared Gulliver's enormous power. Because of this fear, there was neither friendship nor cooperation between them.

But Gulliver? He knew how to promptly persuade perplexed people. He took care not to frighten them with sudden movements as they stood close to him. His pistols and sword were set aside. He assured them of his peaceful intentions. And in his own words, "The natives came by degrees to be less apprehensive of any danger from me. I would sometimes lie down, and let five or six of them dance on my hand. And at last the boys and girls would venture to come and play hide and seek in my hair."

Once the Lilliputians were assured of Gulliver's friendly intentions, they welcomed him as their honored guest.

Here is the vital point we want to make from this story: At the same time that people admire the powerful personality they also tend to be somewhat timid toward him. Because they do not have too much confidence and forthrightness of their own, they do not understand those qualities in another.

If you want to attract and influence people, make it your plan to not only build a strong personality but a *comfortable* one. Let people feel at ease with you. You could take this simple pointer and by working steadily with it you could enormously enrich all your relations with people. You would have more friends and customers and helpers than you would know how to handle. Really.

A comfortable personality is a powerful personality.

In previous pages we have examined human nature to find that people are, in general, more or less timid and apprehensive. They are anxious over the future. They regret the past. They worry over their children and their finances and their place in life. They are jittery. In other words, they are uncomfortable.

People need and need desperately the strong person who can put them at ease. They would give almost anything to find someone who doesn't add to their already heavy burden. They hope to find someone who is strong but who does not frighten them with his strength. "No one loves the man whom he fears." (Aristotle)

As a matter of fact, one of the rarest and most precious of human powers is the ability to remove some of the pressures of everyday living. How can you develop this power for yourself? Largely by practicing a variation of the Golden Rule:

Don't do unto others what they habitually do unto you. This means that we should:

Not expect too much of others.

Not harp on our own troubles endlessly.

Not have critical attitudes toward another.

Not be domineering.

Not ask personal questions.

Not talk depressingly.

Not be unapproachable.

Not put others on the spot.

Not express shock or dismay toward anyone.

Not forget to make ourselves pleasant to be around.

It is important that we become aware of those little things — they are usually little things —which disturb others. The best way to do this is to become alertly aware of the things that make *you* uncomfortable. Notice, for instance, that you prefer that your companions do not talk gloomily or critically.

Get the habit of asking yourself, "Let's see now; how am I affecting this person I am with? Does he appear to be comfortable with me? Am I conversing on a subject of mutual interest? Am I avoiding a critical attitude? Exactly what sort of impression am I making?"

This sort of self-inquiry leads to increased self-awareness, which, in turn, makes you a more comfortable person. That is what your friends want you to be. That is what they like in you.

Moreover, the comfortable personality is one who helps to relieve others of the thousand and one anxieties that fill their daily lives. If you will learn the secret of reducing the tensions of other people you will be an outstanding personality — and a persuasive one. The reduction of anxiety is a major factor in influencing people. Individuals tend to move from an old to a new position whenever a restraining anxiety has been removed. For instance, if you are selling a product or a service to someone, you can not only show him how he will gain by it but also *why he will not suffer any kind of a loss by going ahead.* Prove to him that he is not losing his money, but investing it. Make it clear that he will not suffer loss of his individuality by going along with you; he is really showing good judgment.

Entertainers, such as singers, musicians, and comedians are experts in the art-of-persuasion-through-reduction-of-anxiety. Comedians are well aware that audiences laugh whenever their inner tensions are relieved. Here is a typical comedy stunt which will help you to remember the power of this technique:

The comedian walks onstage carefully balancing a tray upon which is precariously balanced a dozen pyramided bottles. He dances about while skillfully keeping the bottles from tumbling. The audience is tense—will he spill them or not? The anxiety mounts as the entertainer speeds up his dancing pace. The accompanying music grows louder. At the climax of the act the entertainer does a somersault, head over heels—and keeps the bottles upright. As he walks offstage amidst appreciative applause he carelessly lets the tray dangle downward—but the bottles do not fall. They had been nailed to the tray! The audience laughs.

By first building up the anxiety of his audience as to whether or not he would spill the bottles, he was then able to release their tension through laughter. The whole thing was not as dangerous as it looked. What a relief!

In your social relations you need not first build up tensions in other people. They already have them in painful abundance. Your part is to make yourself a comfortable person, one who relaxes and soothes. This is guaranteed to make you a pleasing and welcome personality wherever you go.

Prominent Points for Daily Help

1. Your brighter personality guarantees your richer future. Here you have an exciting motive for uplifting yourself.

2. Everyone has the choice of being a Commander or the Commanded. Stick by your decision to win the magic power to persuade and command people.

3. You charge your personality with extra energy every time you go directly after what you want from life. Have you noticed how the strong individual always seems to know where he's headed?

4. Get the habit of refusing to do things just because they are expected of you. It builds your independence. It commands respect from others, especially from those who make unreasonable demands upon you.

5. Have the courage and the good sense to shed programs and ideas that do nothing for you.

6. Don't meet other people with fixed ideas as to what you should say and do. Practice the technique supplied in this chapter for releasing your vast originalities.

7. Don't underestimate your abilities to build a powerfully persuasive personality. If you think it is impossible, you just think so.

8. Like Gulliver, assure people of your friendly intentions. Sometimes that alone is enough to win their cooperation.

9. Be a comfortable person.

10. The powerful personality is one who recognizes and helps to release the tensions and anxieties of others. Everyone is attracted to the man who helps him feel better.

Chapter 12

TURNING YOUR POWER OVER PEOPLE INTO FINANCIAL GAIN

A number of years ago a very wealthy man told me, "It is just as easy to make 1,000 dollars as it is to make 10 dollars." At that time I didn't believe him. I still don't. I believe it is often much *easier* to earn $1,000 than $10.

That is, when you use your magic power to persuade and command people.

The purpose of this chapter is to show you how you can turn your power over people into additional income and toward career advancement.

The more you master the art of persuading people, the more money you will earn. Nothing is more clearly evident than that. And nothing should excite you quite so much as to realize that your command over people can be turned into command over financial fortune.

I once heard a talk delivered by a prominent banking official before a group of factory employees. The employees had gathered together at lunch time to learn more about the art of earning and investing money. The title of that talk was *People Are Money*. If you are interested in financial advancement, that title should be memorized and repeated constantly by you. The plain fact is, people *are* money, as we shall see in this chapter.

Stop and think for a moment. How do you win a raise in pay? You get it by persuading someone that you are worth that additional sum. How do you attract more clients to your office? By causing them to believe that you are the man who can best serve their interests. In what way do you sell more of your merchandise? By appealing to those drives and urges which motivate people to pay you their cash for your goods.

The fundamental principles for becoming wealthy are certain and they are permanent; being natural laws, they cannot be destroyed. And they persistently offer opportunity to you today. Writing on the subject of how fortunes are made, the famous financial expert Roger W. Babson makes the exciting declaration:

> Though opportunities for service and success have been revolutionized, they have not lessened. They have expanded... hold fast to the old ideals—the ideals of service and reward, of patient probing for facts, of constant flexibility to changing conditions, of timely caution and courage.[26]

I recently ran across a pair of success stories as reported in the newspapers. They so excellently illustrate what we have been talking about that I'd like to pass them on to you.

> Mr. A., a restaurateur, opened an establishment featuring Mexican foods. At first it didn't look like the dining public was much interested in his tamales and enchiladas and tacos; the cash register showed a total of only $460 for his first week of operation. But that was just the first week. Those who dropped in for his tamales soon discovered something else just as spicy. They began telling their friends about that something special.

---

26 Roger W. Babson, *Business Barometers for Profits—Security—Income,* Ninth Edition (New York; Harper and Brothers, 1959).

Their friends dropped in and were soon telling *their* friends about it.

Mr. A's restaurant presently draws in more than a half-million dollars per year. How come? In his interview with newspaper reporters, Mr. A revealed that extra spicy item: "I've developed the ability to treat people as individuals, not just as crowds of customers. For instance, it takes only a split second to drop by a table to ask my diners whether everything is all right. They nod appreciatively and tell me all is fine. That little courtesy turns diners into friends. In other words, I serve them with self-esteem as well as with food. The dinner is as good as they expect, but my personal attention is an unexpected and delightful dessert."

Mr. G., an office worker, wanted to get into business for himself. He thought it just might be possible to turn his hobby into a profitable source of income. His hobby was that of building models of covered wagons. The more he looked at those symbols of the pioneer west the more he was convinced that he could commercialize them. "How," he asked himself, "can I connect covered wagons with a basic human desire? How can I make people want to buy them?" He set his mind to searching for ways to get the covered wagons rolling into homes throughout the country.

One morning he stepped into his front yard and walked to the mailbox. As he leafed through the letters he suddenly froze. Something buzzed inside his mind. That mailbox. Funny, but it had the same general form of a covered wagon. Hmmmmm. Why, he wondered, couldn't a mailbox look like . . . like a covered wagon? That, he excitedly realized, just might be it!

It took no more than a couple of evenings to replace his own metal mailbox with a covered wagon. It attracted instant attention and praise. The next few wagons he built were placed in the window of a local merchant who thought they had possibilities. They had. The merchant placed a hurry-up call for a second order.

That, in brief, is how Mr. G. got into a business that promises to roll along as merrily as a covered wagon. He explains his success like this: "People not only want to be somewhat different from their neighbors, but they want to *display* their uniqueness. Because my covered wagon is something special, it makes its purchaser someone special. That is why he buys."

If you were to study the lives of some of the famous giants of finance you would find that they knew as much about human nature as they did about their specific businesses. Philip Armour, the pioneer meat packer, was one of the first to reward employees for suggestions which broadened his business. This founder of Armour and Company had grasped the powerful secret that individual incentive is fired up by individual reward.

Constantly impress yourself with this absolute fact: *Your money-making capacities will rise rapidly as you master the principles for commanding people.* In my lectures I illustrate this truth by asking the audience to remember the progress of a doubled penny. If you take a single penny and double it each day for 30 days, here is what would happen: At the end of two days you would have, of course, 2 cents; on the third day it would double to 4 cents. Ten days of doubling would give you $5.12; at 15 days you would have $163.84. At 20 days the amount would swell to $5,242.88. At the end of 30 days you would have the magnificent total of $5,368,709.12.

This interesting illustration will help you to remember that as you multiply your skill in handling people, your financial fortunes zoom upward spectacularly.

How to Get Others to Earn Money for You

Half the time that a man thinks he is having business problems he isn't. Not really. He just thinks so. What he is really having is a people problem. By this I mean that he may be:

Failing to call on the right people.

Not offering enough of value to others. Associating with the wrong people.

Not going directly after what he wants. Not contacting enough people.

Failing to draw full benefit from others.

Having negative attitudes toward people.

Not handling people skillfully.

Let that man look beneath the surface of things and he may discover that his real problem lies in his faulty human relations. But because he doesn't realize that this is the case he wrongly concludes that his financial weakness is due to poor business conditions or to stiff competition. (Incidentally, both poor business and competition *can be rubbed out of existence by the determined man who flatly refuses to accept them as necessary blocks.* It is a man's mental acceptance of poverty and limitation that makes them appear. *Refusal* is the magic that causes them to disappear.)

After all, the basic principles of commercial enterprise are familiar to everyone. They are so clearly defined that they offer no problem. All of us know that a profit is earned by buying for $1 and selling for $1.50. It is hardly a secret that you will have more money left over for yourself by eliminating waste and inefficiency in your business practices. You and I are well aware that it pays to advertise. These principles are perfectly clear.

No, it is usually not a violation of the laws of finance that keep a man down. It is almost always a violation of one or more of the laws governing human relations.

What can be done about it?

You can employ the *Three Plan.*

You can expect financial miracles to come your way once you do.

What is the Three Plan?

Very simple. You make it your clear-cut goal to contact a minimum of three people who can contribute in one way or another to your financial enrichment. What you are going to do is to get others to help you make more money. Here are 10 ways to track down your treasures:

1. Set a goal of winning three entirely new customers or clients within a challenging period of time.

2. Study and employ the techniques of three people who have a knack for making money.

3. Ask three experts in your business for suggestions which will promote your prosperity.

4. Select three so-called difficult customers or clients and use your new skills in human relations to sell more of your goods or services.

5. Read three books by authoritative experts which will promote some phase of your business, such as salesmanship or the investment of spare cash.

6. Contact three people who might assist you in gaining a position superior to your present one.

7. Observe the personalities of three people who consistently turn their acts and attitudes into cash.

8. Spend less time with three clients who demand more attention than they are really entitled to.

9. Contact three no-longer-active accounts and work skillfully at reviving them.

10. Select three people and make it your sole business to arouse in them an enthusiasm for your goods or services.

David G. ran a variety store on the boulevard. One day in checking over his stock of merchandise he found himself with 300 hand mirrors on his hands. His choice for action fell on point 3: *Ask three experts in your business for suggestions which will promote your prosperity.*

Among the salesmen who called upon David was a man who magnificently lived up to his title of salesman. He was a live-wire student of human nature who made his study pay personal profit. Deciding to make use of all that valuable knowledge, David came right to the point: "My shelves are stocked with 300 hand-mirrors. How can I sell them?"

"Find some way to connect them with a basic human emotion," the salesman advised. "Don't try to sell the mirrors as mirrors alone. Tie them in with some psychological satisfaction; add something personal. Sell fulfillment of a human need."

David pondered the advice. How could he connect a personal human need with an impersonal piece of glass? How could he get shoppers to see pleasures in his mirrors as well as their reflections? Those were the interesting questions he tackled.

"Well," he finally told himself, "everyone likes to feel *lucky*. Can that pleasurable desire be connected with my mirrors? It's certainly worth an experiment."

Four-leaf clovers he knew, were symbols of good luck. So searching around the store he found a stock of paper ones. He pasted one of the green clovers at the top of a mirror. It looked lucky. He fixed up 50 of the good luck mirrors and displayed them in the main window. In their midst stood a large sign which shouted LUCKY YOU!

David scored a hit. All because everyone *does* want to feel that good fortune is coming his way. It became fashionable for the young folks of the community to carry around good luck mirrors. Every time they looked at themselves they felt freshly fortunate.

That is one example of how you can employ the Three Plan to finance yourself with human nature.

Let's look into the pages of history for an interesting example of point 6: Contact three people who might assist you in gaining a position superior to your present one.

The art of photography was a vigorous infant during the early days of the Civil War. It was a familiar enough profession at that time but there was still ample opportunity for some energetic pioneer to withdraw fame and fortune from his magic box. One of them did.

That alert pioneer was Mathew Brady. He had the photography equipment. He had the skill. Most importantly, he had the initiative.

When war broke out between the states, Brady decided to pursue his profession with as much official backing as possible. No small-minded man, this Mathew Brady. He contacted the most important person in the nation, President Abraham Lincoln. He presented his program to the President with a simple and straightforward request: "I want," Brady's appeal might be summed up, "to adventure with my camera into an historical world—the battlefield."

Lincoln discussed the request with Alan Pinkerton, chief of the United States Secret Service. Brady's persuasiveness prevailed. The President and Pinkerton agreed that he should proceed.

Brady faithfully followed the armies during those years of furious fighting and muddy marching. He shot scenes that today are classics of photography.

Because Mathew Brady sought help from someone who was able to promote him, he won the fame that his initiative deserved. Oh, yes, it was financially profitable, also: The United States government purchased some of his pictures for $25,000.

Get yourself into action with a Three Plan of your own. It cannot fail, in the long run or the short, to yield surprisingly rich results. For one thing, it throws the law of averages **on** your side. Contact enough people and you are bound to score a good percentage of hits. Also, you will find an automatic strengthening of your self-confidence, and that in itself is worth money.

Your Personality and Your $$$

There is excellent reason why the chapter on the enrichment of your personality is placed before this one on financial advancement. Your personality is worth money, and lots of it.

What would you think of a man who started life with no special advantages but who built a career sparkling with the following achievements?

The creator of several financial fortunes.

A friend and advisor to the King of England. A diplomat of skill and power.

A masterful persuader of people.

A charmer of men and women alike.

A pioneer agent in the British Secret Service.

The author of a book which has been a best seller for hundreds of years.

You would probably think that this man's successes were due to his determined and energetic personality.

You would be right.

The name of this bright personality was Daniel Defoe. You probably recognize him as the author of that favorite classic *Robinson Crusoe*.

His achievements are listed to spotlight the fact that your personality has everything to do with anything you do—including your constant customs for collecting comforting cash.

The author of Investments for Professional People points out:

> Regardless of the profession a man has selected or whether he has chosen to pursue it independently or within an organization, a large measure of his ultimate success will depend upon his personality . . . The man who has learned to appraise his fellow citizens and evince a genuine interest in them will not fail in his chosen profession . . . Their possession will pay rich dividends throughout the years, both in tangible financial rewards and in such valuable intangible benefits as friendship and esteem.[27]

> Not long ago I was in the office of an attorney to discuss some legal papers connected with a real estate transaction. That lawyer apparently had everything it took to build a prosperous career. He had the education and a good mind to go with it. His office was modern and impressive. He also had an intense desire to win a name for himself. He had just about every-thing—except the most essential element of all. Knowing that I wrote and lectured on personal problems, he asked, "What is the matter with me? Why don't I attract more clients?"

> "Because," I told him, "they don't believe that you can help them."

> "What do you mean? I'm a qualified lawyer. I have my degrees. I'm efficient. I win cases."

> "If you don't mind me saying so, you didn't win me when I came in here."

> "Oh? Tell me why not. I can take it."

27 Robert U. Cooper, M.D., *Investments for Professional People*, Rev. Ed. (New York: The Macmillan Company, 1959). Reprinted by permission of the publisher.

"Well, look. I came in here needing your forthright guidance. I expected you to take instant command, to act in a positive, authoritative manner, to appear to know exactly what to do. Instead . ."

"You mean my personality lacks a show of strength?"

"I wanted you to *assure* me that you knew your business. I failed to get that assurance."

"How did I fail to come through?"

"In little things. Instead of giving me your alert attention, your eyes wandered worriedly over some papers on your desk. You didn't show an aggressive interest by asking vital questions. You seemed generally hesitant."

'In other words, my personality was too negative."

"Your awareness of your lack is a long step in itself toward correction. You *may* be an expert when it comes to handling my business, but í *don't know that.* You have to sell me on yourself. You are in charge of operations around here. *Take* charge. I guarantee your flourishing fortunes."

Want to build a money-making personality the easy way? Then remember, "Responsibility walks hand in hand with capacity and power." (J. G. Holland)

At one time I needed someone to do some rapid editorial work on a manuscript that was due at the publisher very shortly. I offered the task to three different men. Two of them *thought* they could do the work, they *hoped* I would be pleased with results, and *wondered* if I could extend them additional time should it become necessary.

The third man set the manuscript under his arm, strode to the door, turned and told me, "Mr. Howard, I know that you want fast and accurate work on this. It will be done. You can rest your mind about it. I'll take total charge for doing things up right. The manuscript will be back in your hands within three days. Good-bye." With a friendly wave he briskly turned and left.

There was a responsible man. He took charge. Right now. He also had that valuable ability to put himself into the other man's shoes. He not only knew what I wanted from him but had the astuteness to reassure me on the outcome of the work. His positive manner rested my mind completely. I knew I could depend upon him. That man easily influenced me into wanting to do more business with him. I haven't the slightest doubt but that he has long since advanced to a position of power in the business world. With a forthright willingness like that, no man could possibly fall short of his aims.

Here is one way to achieve maximum effectiveness: Always assume that your personality is not glowing as brightly as it might. This is really a positive attitude, not a negative one, for it tends to prod you upward and above your present level.

An acquaintance of mine is one of the most masterful after-dinner speakers in his city. His audiences demand him back time after time. He got to that popular position by asking himself, at the end of each talk, just how he could have sharpened things. Bit by bit his shortcomings as a speaker dropped away, to be replaced by wit and a convincing manner. That man has earned the right to be proud of himself and his speeches.

In a class I once conducted we used to ask the students to write down a single goal which they wanted to achieve. They were next asked to list three definite courses of action which, when taken, would help make the goal a reality. Finally, they were asked to write down either *yes* or *no* in answer to whether or not they were willing to take personal responsibility for carrying out those three actions. Those who answered *yes*—as did almost all—achieved their aims with far less difficulty than they had thought possible.

What is a good definition of self-responsibility? Here is a very simple one which serves excellently: It is the courageous willingness to personally take hold of a situation and do what has to be done with it.

Let's illustrate one way in which this power can help you win others over to your side of the fence: Many people find it almost torturous to make up their minds. Even such little things as which dress to wear or what supper to prepare plunges them into inner conflict. Also, they don't want to take the consequences of a wrong decision. Therefore, if you can assure them that you will stand responsible for the results of their decision they will be far more inclined to go along with you. Business firms know the value of this device; that is why they offer money-back guarantees.

If you reply to this, "Yes, but maybe I don't want to take the responsibility," then I say that you should not be trying to persuade the particular person involved in it. We must extend a certain measure of responsibility toward anyone whom we are trying to influence. Willingness to do so indicates personal strength, and without that quality we won't be very persuasive anyway.

Answer with an unconditional *yes* to additional responsibility. That is how you can turn your personality into a cash income.

Scientific Systems for Financial Gain

Some unwise people permit others to create financial problems for them. You can be wiser than that. Use the following ideas for permitting others not only to solve your problems but to contribute to your positive enrichment. These ideas are called scientific because that is what they are. Each is based on tested and proven principles governing human nature as it relates to money-making.

1. A PROFITABLE SUGGESTION

The power of the simple suggestion was illustrated to me recently while chatting with a chief of police.

"Notice," he remarked, "what happens when you are waiting in your car at a red traffic signal. If you edge your car forward a few inches, the man in the next car will quite likely do likewise. Your inching forward suggests to him that he had better follow your lead in getting ready to go."

Whatever your business or profession may be, the simple power of suggestion plays its profitable role every day. Your advertisement is a suggestion that people should buy your goods or engage your services. Your efficiency at your office desk or in the factory is a type of suggestion that you are worth your wages and maybe even more.

The point is, make full use of your power of positive suggestion. It is as subtle as it is effective. Find as many ways as you can to suggest to the other man that he needs whatever you have to offer. Also suggest that he will be delighted with it.

Remember, *people want you to convince them of their reward.* They always welcome any suggestion that promises personal progress.

2. BE ALERT TO ADVERTISING METHODS

A salesman was seated before his television set enjoying an evening of relaxation. As a commercial message came on he found himself listening with alert curiosity. There was something about the appeal that made him want to pay attention. Thinking he might be on the edge of a valuable technique which could be applied to his own sales-program, he studied the message. It was based, he saw, on the human desire to *save* something, to avoid unnecessary time and trouble.

His discovery delighted him, for it was one that could easily be applied to his own business. He decided that from that day forward he would strengthen his persuasions by showing customers how his products could save them time, money, effort, energy, distress, disappointment, and so forth.

Make it your habit to study commercial advertising. Select helpful techniques and transfer them to your own program. Notice how these expertly prepared messages appeal to and satisfy basic human needs. That is why they are just right for your own money-making ventures.

3.   MAINTAIN YOUR SELF-VALUE

The German philosopher Friedrich von Schiller once declared, "Every man stamps his value on himself." Now then, it is a well-established psychological principle that people will value you at just about the same level as you value yourself. If you want to influence others favorably, price yourself and your services at a reasonably high level. People prefer to associate with quality. They admire the man who maintains his integrity. They are attracted to the personality who calmly affirms his own self-worth.

Some people tend to give themselves away too cheaply. They do this in the hope of attracting gratitude and appreciation, but it actually produces the opposite effect. It is a fact about human nature that a man appreciates something in proportion to his payment for it.

As an example of this, a friend of mine used to give free talks and lectures. Although he was a lively speaker, he never received more than the usual polite thanks for his efforts. Finally deciding that his time had a commercial value, he set a reasonable fee for his platform appearances. Now he not only receives his fee, but finds his audiences much more appreciative.

Summary: Value yourself highly. Others will do likewise.

Summary of Your Money-Making Methods

1. The art of persuading people guarantees your rich financial future. Become an artist.

2. Remember that all your money-making ventures involve other people. The secret of success is to involve yourself in a way that persuades them to follow you.

3. Any correction you make in your human relations cannot fail to return a sizeable profit to you, both financially and in personal happiness.

4. Employ the *Three Plan*. Use the listed ten ways, also, write down and work out those that apply to your specific needs.

5. Remember that your personality is always worth $$$$. Blend the ideas of Chapter 11 with this chapter. The combination is power-packed.

6. A strong and confident personality makes a major contribution to business achievement. Everyone wants to do business with the man who is sure of himself.

7. One of the most attractive of all personality traits *is* that of self-responsibility. The more you have of that admirable trait, the more you attract favorable attention from those who can advance you.

8. Experiment with the simple power of suggestion. It is a subtle force that works more often than realized.

9. Maintain a sense of self-worth. Others will value you accordingly.

10. The way to wealth-through-people is certain, permanent, and honorable. All it takes is your persistent exploration.

ANSWERS TO YOUR QUESTIONS
ABOUT WINNING YOUR WAY

You might as well win personal power the easy way. The following questions and answers will save effort and energy as you go about your people-persuading plans. Over the years I have found them to be among the most-often-asked. Apply the answers to your own programs.

The Power of Self-Awareness

"AT A LOS ANGELES LECTURE I HEARD YOU SPEAK
ON THE INFLUENTIAL POWER OF SELF-AWARENESS.
WILL YOU PLEASE REVIEW?"

Self-awareness results from honest self-observation. The person who wishes to discover his real self should look at himself to find out what is true, not merely what he wants to be true. This means that we should become aware of our daily thoughts and motives, of our feelings and our attitudes, and especially of our rationalizations. The human mind is a tricky thing; it tries desperately to escape from whatever it doesn't care to face about itself. As a humorous example, the foreman of a building project asked a worker, "How come you're carrying only one board when the others are handling two?" After thinking it over, the worker came up with the perfect rationalization, "It must be because they are too lazy to make two trips like I do."

Some people make the mistake of thinking that realistic observation of themselves means that they should be grim or pessimistic about it. Not at all. It is perfectly possible to be earnest in your self-searching without being gloomy. The reality of your life is that you *can* grow in strength and in security, that you *are* able to change your personality and your circumstances, that opportunities *do* exist bountifully, that riches and respect *can* appear before the man who knows how to turn his personal power into a successful life.

These are the cheery realities. All else is mistaken viewpoint.

Let me tell you a story that shows how self-understanding can make others appreciate you:

One afternoon I was driving the highway while accompanied by a salesman with whom I was doing business. I asked him to supply me with some details concerning our transaction, which he proceeded to do. As we approached the business district the traffic grew heavier, which required that I pay more attention to my driving and less to the conversation. However, we continued to talk. The traffic finally got so confused that I had to set my whole mind on safe driving—and at that point the salesman remarked with a grin, "I see that you have your hands full with the traffic. I'll keep quiet until we're in the clear."

It suddenly struck me that he had really said something quite unusual. It was rare that a passenger had the insight to realize that I couldn't concentrate on both driving and listening at the same time. I appreciated that man's thoughtfulness immensely.

"How come," I asked him later, "you realized that I had all I could handle in the traffic?"

"Because," he replied, "I was aware of how *I* would feel in the same situation."

Self-awareness supplies you with other-awareness. And other-awareness gives you power, influence — and quite often some delightful appreciation from others.

The Chronically Antagonistic Person

"A Number Of Us Work Alongside A Chronically Antagonistic Person. Will You Comment Generally On The Problem?"

You sometimes run into people who are incapable of normal give-and-take in human relations. Emotional wounds from bitter experiences of the past prevent them from accepting much in the way of love or friendship or even relaxed companionship. Such people are apt to be hostile and suspicious to your suggestions which would do them some good. They keep you at arm's length. The truth is, you waste your time and energy trying to reach such people by direct effort. They have locked the door, and woe unto anyone who approaches with a key.

Such a person often gives the *appearance* of getting better. One day he shows up so radiantly gay that you wonder whether the long-awaited improvement has at last taken place. But come next day and his usual miserable self reappears. It always does, sooner or later, because no *basic* betterment has really taken place in his personality. He is cheery merely because something from outside himself excites his feelings or tickles his fancy. If you take a bowl of water and splash it back and forth inside the bowl, it will rise briefly to above-usual heights on the sides of the bowl. But once your outside energy disappears, it falls back to its usual level. That illustrates one characteristic of this kind of person. I guess you could call him a splash in the pan.

Another characteristic of such problem-people is their excessive need to blame others for their own predicament. I recall a humorous incident which illustrates a philosophic attitude which will help you in dealing with them:

It was pickup day and my neighbor dutifully deposited her boxes of trash near the curb. As she turned back toward her house a nervous yellow mongrel shoved his nose eagerly into the boxes, scattering trash all over the sidewalk. Shooed away from his hoped-for meal, Fido insisted on yapping angrily from a safe distance. As she patiently picked up the papers, my neighbor calmly eyed the snapping mongrel, then addressed him with the kindly philosophic words, "I don't think you understand. *I'm* the one who's supposed to bark."

Most of all, chronically antagonistic people need your understanding, for they have none of their own. They just cannot see how things really are. Here is where your philosophic patience becomes a good tool for persuading them toward cooperation. Just let them go their troubled way. Be nice to them and let them go at that. In time they may return of their own free will to give you another opportunity to show them that you like them after all.

Don't forget this golden rule when dealing with such a person, male or female: Once you reach him through the proper secret passage, he will go all out to harmonize with you. He holds a hidden welcome sign which he will gladly show whomever first wins his confidence.

The Role of Appearance in Persuasion

"I'm Afraid I'm Not Quite The Handsomest Man In Town. What Part Does Physical Appearance Play In Person-To-Person Persuasion?"

None. Beyond the usual requirements of personal neatness and good grooming, we can look exactly like nature made us and use it to positive advantage when with other people.

In the first chapter of this book I promised to prove to you that personal persuasiveness does not depend upon us looking like something out of the latest Hollywood epic. I bring this matter up because lots of people think that it does. It doesn't. Think of some of the influential people in the public eye and you will agree that physical perfection has nothing to do with personal power and social charm.

A man is appealing to others according to what he is, not according to what he looks like. The things that count are a man's personality, his talents as a leader, and his ability to inspire and help those who know him. People don't really care whether or not their leader is the handsomest man in town, but it is important to them that he be a strong leader. *People are interested in what another can do for them.* A thirsty man hasn't the slightest concern with what the drinking glass looks like.

Dr. Camilla M. Anderson points out, ". . . the psychological person rather than the physical person determines most behavior."[28]

This means that your behavior is based on your inner qualities. If your inner self is attractive it will automatically produce attractive behavior toward others. And pleasing acts and words are really the persuasive forces that sway people your way.

Besides. . .

When is a man handsome?

When is a woman beautiful?

I will tell you:

When someone says so. You are handsome or you are beautiful because someone else thinks you are. When either quality is attributed to you, it becomes a fact with you. The fact that someone thinks you are attractive is the whole matter; nothing else is valid, not even what you think about it. *Proof:* If another person thinks you are attractive, and you disagree with him, your negative opinion makes no difference to the other person. He sees what he sees and likes what he sees and we can all be very happy about that.

---

28 *Saints, Sinners and Psychiatry,* by Camilla M. Anderson, M.D. Paperback Ed., The Durham Press, Portland, Ore., 1962.

You can make anyone think that you are handsome or that you are beautiful. And once you do you really are. As a matter of fact, you were quite attractive all along. You just didn't believe it.

Knowing the Needs of Others

"I REALIZE THAT SUCCESSFUL PERSUASION
IS BASED ON SUPPLYING THE NEEDS OF OTHERS.
HOW CAN I TELL WHAT THEY WANT?"

By becoming aware of your own needs and tastes. This is so important a point that it has been emphasized throughout this book.

Basically, we all want the same things, such as security, a feeling of self-esteem, someone to encourage our efforts. Your clear awareness of your needs is an accurate method of realizing what the other person wants. People who do not understand themselves have a lesser capacity for understanding others. Because they cannot accurately identify their own yearnings, they cannot recognize the longings of others— and hence cannot supply them. Self-knowledge always has been and always will be the guide to knowledge of others.

The story goes about a young pharmacist and his bride who visited some relatives on a New Jersey farm. During the conversation they were served with a newly delicious cold beverage. It was like nothing the young couple had tasted before. The pharmacist learned that it had been brewed from a variety of roots and barks which grew in the surrounding woods. The young man began to wonder, "If *I* like this unusual beverage, wouldn't others like it too?"

Upon arriving home, he began to experiment in creating his own special beverage. For flavoring he used the roots and herbs from the shelves of his drug store. He served the finished drink to some of his customers. They liked it—immensely. It tasted just as delicious to them as it did to the man who made it.

With mounting enthusiasm, the pharmacist mixed more roots and barks. The more he mixed the more he sold. It wasn't long before his delicious beverage was occupying most of his business hours.

That, in brief, is how a famous root beer manufacturing firm—the Charles E. Hires Company—got its start. Young Charles E. Hires wisely realized that something that tasted special to *him* might also taste special to others. His psychology was correct and his ambitious experiments proved it.

The thing to do is to build a "want consciousness." This means that you become increasingly aware of the needs and tastes and desires of other people. There is no better way to do this than to experiment with human nature as you go about your daily affairs. Select three or four people whom you meet and observe their personalities. Ask yourself, "Just what kind of a person is he? What seems to be his most basic needs? To be praised for his work? To be set at ease with me? To have a receptive ear whenever he has something to say? To be encouraged in this or that?"

As you practice this, you will find an unexpectedly interesting thing happening. You will become more and more aware of your *own* needs, for you will be seeing basic human nature. You will begin to truly find yourself, to observe yourself with clarity of thought. And *that* is when you really empower yourself, for once you clearly know what you want, you will have no trouble at all in getting it from others.

Personality Growth

**"I Feel That My Personality Is Not Growing
As Energetically As It Might.
Will You Please Offer A Solution?"**

If you will really carry out the following plan, you will energize every department of your life:

Don't be afraid to sever unprofitable relationships.

It could be a business account that costs more than it pays; maybe it's a friendship of doubtful value; perhaps you are wasting your time with this club or that activity. If you are not really getting what you want and need from a particular association, why continue it? It just doesn't make sense to waste abilities that could well be directed toward self-advancement. Take a look at your relationships. If you feel doubtful about some of them, even resentful, consider that they had better be severed and replaced. "In all societies, it is advisable to associate with the highest..." (Colton)

Richard A., who ran a retail business of his own, dropped in to ask, "Why don't I attract more profitable relations? Is my personality keeping me from meeting more people and enjoying more success with them? Why don't I win what I want from people?"

"Because," I told him, "you are compromising. And you compromise because you don't know any better. The reason you are not getting what you want from your social relationships is because in your heart of hearts you mistakenly feel that you are now getting all that there is to get. You don't like that limitation but you foolishly accept it. You cling to what little you have for fearing of losing all. Why do you mistakenly believe that there is only one job or one lady friend or one social circle? Who told you that? Why all this gullible belief in scarcity?"

"What," Richard asked, "has that to do with my personality?"

"Everything destructive. Each day that you tolerate an unfair or unprofitable relationship you reinforce your false conviction that that is the best you can do. And that, believe me, is what causes a personality to suffer and wither."

"So what do I do?"

"Be willing to cut yourself adrift from whatever shaky support your present associations give you. Don't worry about finding better people or superior circumstances. They exist. You just don't know them as yet. But you will. America was here long before Columbus discovered it. But first he had to sail away from Spain."

Look at your own associations and contacts. Are some of them more habitual than profitable? If so, have the courage to sail away to new and refreshing worlds.

Making Others Understand

"How Can I Make The Other Person Understand Things Quickly?"

By dealing with him on *his* terms of understanding. Here is a place where many persuaders, even the experts, falter in their programs. It is all too easy to forget that while *we* may know what is going on, the other person may be removed mentally 10 blocks away.

You must remember that *his* mind is not *your* mind. Therefore he won't and can't see things as you do.

The story is told of the doctor who prescribed all sorts of pills and liquids to a businessman patient who complained of sleepless nights. None worked. Upon the patient's next visit the good doctor gave him an album of phonograph records, thinking that soft music might soothe the man into dreamland. A recording of Vienna waltzes failed, as did one consisting of peaceful symphonies. After carefully thinking about his patient's background, the doctor gave him a record carrying the repeated sound of a clanging cash register. That did it! That was something that businessman understood!

In order that you might understand this idea as clearly as possible, let me tell you something about the human mind and how it operates: The mind is absolutely incapable of understanding anything above its own level. If people do not understand you, the simple reason is that no man can understand something which is beyond his own experience. (This is why it is pointless to argue or plead with a person who resists understanding any particular truth. He *can't* understand because he *won't* understand.)

In a recent group discussion I illustrated this idea by setting four human figures on a map of the United States. The figures were set in the center of the map, backs to each other, each facing one of the four directions of north, south, east, west. This illustration helped to get over the point that everyone you meet is as different in his personal viewpoints as he is in his physical appearance. Each sees the world according to the position he faces, that is, according to his beliefs, opinions, and convictions. Therefore, a man facing north is bound to have difficulty appreciating the cotton fields of the South. The man facing east could be told about the wonders of the Rocky Mountains, but he must see them himself in order to really understand their mightiness.

The authors of *Social Psychology* make the point, "One cannot motivate a man to act by using terms outside his comprehension: one must appeal to purposes which he understands and which make sense to him."[29]

To persuade the other person quickly, ask yourself whether you are persuading him in terms of his understanding. Here are five excellent questions to ask yourself:

1. Does he understand the benefits he will receive?

2. Am I using language which he easily grasps?

3. Am I persuading according to his self-interest?

---

29 Alfred R. Lindesmith and Anselm L. Strauss, *Social Psychology*, Rev. Ed. (New York: Holt, Rinehart and Winston, Inc., 1956).

4.   Does he realize what his refusal will cost him?

5.   Is he confused on any point at all?

Get into some personal practice by thinking of someone whom you are trying to win, perhaps a client or friend or child. List some actions you can take which will make your plan clearer to him. Now carry them out. See how much sooner you get both his understanding and his agreement.

1.   _____

2.   _____

3.   _____

4.   _____

5.   _____

Opportunities for Exerting Influence

"What About Opportunities For Exerting Influence And Leadership? Where Do They Exist?"

Wherever there are human beings with human desires. Let's look at the need for *personal participation.* So very many people feel left out of life's best experiences, passed by, ignored. This they don't like. Any of us would rather attend a sizzling barbecue than read about it.

Susie: In this world there's a man for every girl and a girl for every man. Isn't that something to shout about?

Betty: I don't want to shout about it; I just want to get in on it.

This human need for participation, to *live* life is your opportunity for influence. The conversationalist who can include others in the discussion is bound to be popular. The businessman who knows how to set his customers in the center of his advertising will surely see good results in his cash register. The parents who permit their children to share reasonably in family planning will certainly win the affection of the young ones.

Here is an interesting story from the pages of history which shows how one man became wealthy and famous when he took the opportunity to supply another kind of human need:

> A certain British clerk in a government office believed that his fellow countrymen had a need for adding romance and adventure to their lives. He decided to supply this need by writing exciting novels. His first book was such a smashing success that the reading public set up a clamor for more of the same. For over 12 years this imaginative man turned out stirring tales that carried readers away from their dull lives for a while to lift them to worlds of romance and conquest. Curiously enough, no one knew who the author was, for the man behind the pen left his manuscripts unsigned. Today we know that the man who so skillfully fulfilled the human need for escape to glory was Sir Walter Scott, author of *Ivanhoe* and *Kenilworth.*

Remember that people who want things habitually look to a leader who can help to obtain them. Here is how Dr. Harry Emerson Fosdick expresses it:

We love to be mastered ... to feel awe in the presence of commanding personality, to fall in love until we become humble suppliants for the favors of the adored . . . The ability to follow leadership is basic in all hopes of a better world . . . [30]

Opportunities? Limitless. Really.

---

30 Harry Emerson Fosdick, *On Being a Real Person* (New York: Harper and Brothers, Publishers, 1943).

Persuading a Problem Person

"My Usual Attempts To Persuade A Problem Person Get Me Nowhere. What Can I Do?"

Do something different: Ask the problem person himself what would persuade him.

A chief value of this unusual technique is that it comes as a pleasant surprise to the other man. He may be identifying you as an opponent or possibly as someone who is trying to get him to do something contrary to his own wishes. By asking for his assistance, the relationship no longer consists of two opposing wills but rather becomes a situation wherein two minds are earnestly working together to find a mutually beneficial solution. Your identity changes from that of someone who is trying to get something from him to one who is attempting to give him something in exchange for his agreement. This will strike him as being a reasonable bargain to which he can safely give his cooperation.

Also, whenever you ask for his suggestions you get a clearer idea of the kind of reward he expects from his cooperation. If you can supply it, he is sold on the spot.

The story goes about the Indian brave who was hunting in the forest when he came upon a fellow tribesman who was standing silently motionless in back of a big rock.   The brave invited his silent friend, "Come hunting with me. We'll share our bag of game."

"Don't want to," was the stubborn reply.

"The hunting is good today," the brave urged. "Come along."

"Not interested," came the gruff refusal.

In one more desperate attempt the brave enthused, "Think of all the glory well share when we return with a feast."

"No," the motionless Indian scowled.

"What can I do," the brave finally asked, "to talk you into coming with me?"

His friend tilted his head in deep thought for a moment, then answered, "I think I know how you can persuade me."

"How?" inquired the delighted brave.

The motionless Indian pointed down to his feet which were hidden by the rock, then sadly sighed, "Get me out of this bear trap!"

The moral is, ask an obstinate man how you can persuade him. He may give you a surprisingly simple solution.

How to be More Persistent

> **"I WORK AT WINNING WORTHWHILE GOALS WITH OTHER PEOPLE, BUT I GET EASILY DISTRACTED AND DISCOURAGED. HOW CAN I BE MORE PERSISTENT?"**

Place your objective before everything else.

In Chapter 1 we found that we must have clear-cut goals when it comes to winning people. In other words, we must know exactly what we want. That is half the battle. The other half is this:

Set that objective before all else. And you will have it.

The newspapers recently reported the adventure of a man who set out alone in a California desert to seek one of the legendary lost gold mines of the area. While poking around he got lost. He stumbled beneath the burning sun for three days, only to find himself wandering in a circle. With water almost gone he despaired of ever reaching safety. He finally sighted a thin spiral of smoke on the distant horizon. Setting his eye on that smoke he worked his way toward it. He slipped in the sand and he fell over rocks and he got tired and discouraged—but he set his goal before everything else. He made it to that smoke which meant an occupied cabin and safety.

No matter how desperate the circumstances, anyone can have anything he wants — *when* he makes it his first and last order of business.

Whatever your objective with people, you should:

Think about it constantly.

Go after it in one way or another every day.

Refuse to accept your own doubts that you can have it.

Do these things and you will have it.

When driving your car you don't stop when you see a red traffic light a block ahead. You keep going because you know that by the time you get there it will turn green for you. Your continued advance toward that signal is what brings the two of you together favorably. So it is in your social relations. There is never a need to halt in dismay, for your courageous forward movement will surely carry you to the point where you have the green light, to where you pass through to power and happiness in all your human relations.

Important Answers to Remember

1. Learn as much about yourself as you can. You will like what you find. Also, self-awareness is a tremendous force for winning others to your way.

2. Remember that people are attracted to the way a per son acts, not necessarily to the way he looks. Charm is the lasting kind of attractiveness, and anyone can be charming.

3. Experiment with people as a means of building your social effectiveness. Seek to understand them better.

4. Do not hesitate to cut yourself away from unprofitable people and places. Your progress depends upon it. Your first duty is toward yourself.

5. Remember that the other person lives in an entirely different mental world than yours. In all your people-persuading programs, make sure he understands the benefits of going your way.

6. Think of as many ways as possible to offer personal participation to the other person. People like to be actively engaged with life.

7. Your opportunities for leadership and authority are really as limitless as you make them. Why limit yourself?

8. When dealing with a hesitant person, show him that you are giving him something, not taking.

9. Place your goal before everything else. Permit absolutely nothing to interfere with it.

10. Continue your drive toward power and influence. As long as you are moving forward, you cannot fail to reach your desired destination.

Chapter 14

HOW TO EXPAND
YOUR PERSONAL INFLUENCE
OVER PEOPLE

A highly successful man once told me, "Whenever the experts used to tell me that I could achieve ten times as much as I thought I could, I used to think that they said it just to make me feel good. Now I know the real reason they said it—because it's absolutely true. I know. I've proved it in both my business affairs and in my social life."

You can have ten times more of *anything* that you have at the present time. This includes money. It certainly includes peace of mind—also love. It includes everything which you now possess in limited quantity but which you want to enlarge.

By expanding your personal influence with people you can change your life spectacularly. This is true. It is not just something that we want to be true. It is not something we hope is true. It is not just something that Vernon Howard says is true. It is simply true. The fantastic fact merely awaits your discovery.

Down in the South American country of Ecuador the natives keep a sharp lookout on the beaches. Gold coins from sunken treasure ships are washed ashore constantly. Those alert people find treasures because they are watching for them. So you can find your treasures by remaining alert to the opportunities that people constantly send your way.

The plain and regrettable fact is that the man who wants

things from other people barely scratches the surface of his possibilities. His thinking confines itself to a limited circle because he mistakenly believes that the only opportunities that exist are those that he can presently see. With that negative attitude he is hardly in a position to spot those gold coins that could be his own.

The salesman reaches a bare portion of the customers that could be on his list were he to use some new techniques that carry him beyond his current thinking patterns. The man who wishes new ideas for improving his business or personal life hasn't the slightest idea of the extended worlds that lie beyond his vision but not beyond his attainment. In matters of romance, one investigation by a psychologist showed that the average male ventured no more than 14 blocks beyond his own home in search of a marriage mate.

Why don't people get one-tenth of their possibilities? Because they live and move on Friday in the very same routine way that they lived and moved on the preceding Tuesday and Wednesday and Thursday. Happily, anyone who really wants to break through to new worlds of accomplishment can do so with astonishing ease.

One way for crashing through is to make up your mind that you are all through with self-limitation.

Don't limit yourself. Never fall into the trap of believing that what you want must necessarily come from this or that particular person. It just isn't so, even though you may insist upon it. A man thinks in this limited fashion because he confuses familiarity with certainty; he mistakenly thinks that just because this *known* person has what he needs, then this known person is the *only* one who has it. That kind of thinking is just as foolish as declaring that the single ship we see on the ocean is the only ship at sea.

In human relations, people deliberately make themselves believe that another person is wonderfully exclusive; they do this because they deeply yearn to believe in someone who is stronger or wiser or nicer than anyone they have ever met. This prevents them from venturing forth to discover a new acquaintance who is just as nice as the original person and maybe even nicer.

How would you apply these ideas to a practical matter of life, for example, to your finances? Like this: Never believe that your increase must necessarily come from this client or from that method of advertising or from this employer or from that use of your talents. This kind of disbelief frees you to believe accurately, that is, in the financial expansion that lies just beyond you.

Perhaps you remark, "But what about my abilities to expand my personal influence in the world of people? Do I have them in the first place? If so, won't I wear myself out in excessive use? Exactly how can I build my capacities for authority and leadership?"

These are good questions. The answers are just as good. We will let Dr. Erich Fromm take over. He starts off by speaking about those who habitually limit themselves:

> These people tend to feel that they possess only a fixed quantity of strength, energy, or mental capacity, and that this stock is diminished or exhausted by use and can never be replenished. They cannot understand the self-replenishing function of all living substance and that activity and the use of one's powers increase strength . . ,[31]

With fresh confidence in something better and something beyond, let's next attach ourselves to some practical plans for expanding our personal influence.

---

31 Erich Fromm, *Man for Himself* (New York: Holt, Rinehart and Winston, Inc., 1947).

Speech Secrets With Some
Surprising Rewards

I would like to challenge you to do something with the following secrets for persuasive speech. Do this: Select any one of them and dedicate yourself to it for a single week. Read it over several times a day, remind yourself of it constantly, and especially put its message into practice wherever you mingle with people. The next week, do likewise with another selection. Things will happen. Good things. The first thing that will happen is that you will find yourself influencing others in a new and gratifying manner.

The second result is surprising—and extra rewarding. *You will find that you are influencing yourself toward additional confidence and clarity of action.* These pointers have been designed to help you understand yourself as well as the other person. Work with them and you will have double enrichment.

1. The legend goes that James McNeil Whistler, the famous artist, was once sketching an outdoor scene when a friend passed by. Whistler asked his friend how he liked the painting. The visitor looked over the yellow meadows and green woods with only casual interest. Whistler, who had a sharp mind, told him, "Let me show you how I can make this the most fascinating picture you have ever seen." With a few skilled strokes the great artist added something to the canvas. The visitor leaned forward, studied the painting eagerly, smiled and exclaimed, "You are right. You have placed *me* in the picture."

    Get the habit of including others in your conversational canvases. Bring up topics of interest to both of you. Ask them questions, draw out their opinions. Who knows, some of their ideas may be as brilliant as your own!

2. "Gentle words, quiet words, are after all, the most powerful words. They are most convincing, more compelling, more prevailing." (Washington Gladden)

3. I once saw a training film produced for the purpose of showing businessmen ways to become more efficient in the office by building a more harmonious home life.

   In one of the scenes, an executive arrived home in the evening, gave his wife an affectionate kiss, held her back at arm's length, then smilingly told her, "I know something nice about you." While she melted in his arms, he told her several nice things about herself.

   At the conclusion of the film, the man sitting next to me exclaimed, "Wow, what a way to win a wife! *I know something nice about you!*"

   There is no more simple nor intelligent way to become a zestful speaker than to observe those impressive words and phrases used successfully by others. If you are influenced by another's selection of words, it is most likely that you can use those same words to persuade others. Not that you will imitate another, of course; the idea is to become aware of the type of speech that hits the mark. Your very awareness supplies you with new and natural word-power.

4. Use tactful suggestions to influence those who carelessly impose upon you. One businessman avoids last-minute demands upon his time by remarking, "If you will let me know of your need a few hours in advance, I can set the time aside for you especially."

5. Thousands of years ago a Greek poet named Menander set down six words of immense wisdom which are just

as true today as in his time. He wrote: "Nothing is more useful than silence."

You can use silence for studying the other man. Once you get to know how he works you can effectively work him around to your side of the fence.

Silence sets a trap for the unreasonable or unkind individual. Never contradict an obstinate person; just let him talk long enough and he'll contradict himself.

Silence keeps you from saying the wrong thing or the empty or ineffectual thing.

When you silently listen to the other man you extend him a courtesy he won't forget. At the time of your courtesy he will not be aware of it, for he is too busy talking, but when he goes away with a good feeling of being released from some of his pressures, he will like you for permitting him that good feeling.

"After speech, silence is the greatest power in the world." (Lacordaire)

6. Don't let a person with a sober or expressionless face scare you off from speaking to him. He or she is probably using the expression—or lack of it—as a mask for timidity. He is the very one who yearns most of all for you to speak to him; so do so. You yourself have noticed how quickly the atmosphere warms up once the conversation gets going. The shy ones are excellent practice for your program of winning others to you.

7. Make sure that you make yourself understood to the other man. Get your meaning over to him. A man who is confused about your program is not inclined to accept it. Speak to him in simple and easy-to-understand terms.

People are both smarter than you think they are and thicker than you think they are. They are shrewd enough when the matter on hand does not involve their emotions or convictions. Once personal feelings or cherished beliefs enter the picture, they tend to weaken a person's judgments and reasonings. (Now you know why we find it so easy to advise the other person on his problems but get so mixed up with our own!)

Always explain your program several times and in several ways. This assists you in getting around the other man's fixed opinions and it helps him to get your point.

There is one language you can speak which is always understood and appreciated by everyone: It is that of self-advancement. We all want to rise to higher stations and to have more of the good things life holds out to us. So ask yourself whether your man clearly understands all that he will gain from going along with you. Watch the growth of your influence with the person who sees how much he profits from agreeing with you.

8.   "In conversation, avoid the extremes of forwardness and reserve." (Cato)

9.   I was calling on a friend at his furniture store when he brought out two signs, one reading SORRY, WE'RE CLOSED, and the other reading the single word CLOSED.

'Which is best?" he asked me. "I like the one with the *sorry* in it. It seems politer."

"Toss it out," I advised. "Use the single word *closed*."

"Why?" he protested. "Isn't the other one more courteous?"

"You have to understand how some people react," I told him. "When you tell them that your shop is *closed*, that ends the matter right there; they have no emotional responses. But when you tell them that you are *sorry* they react, 'I don't want you to be sorry; I want you to be open when I need you.' They tend to turn your attempt at courtesy against you. They are not conscious that this is their hostile response, for it happens at a deep level of mind, but that is what they are thinking."

The point is: Don't let your spoken words label you as having an apologetic nature. Watch out that you do not overdo such words as "Please" and "I'm sorry" and even "Thank you." People sometimes interpret the use of these words as weakness. And, sad to state, some people tend to take advantage of any supposed weakness in another.

10. In some countries with a chronic fuel shortage it is the custom to heat only one room of the house. By this act of concentration they accomplish their purpose of keeping everyone comfortable.

Do likewise by concentrating all your words on your goal. Don't wander off into trivialities; don't let the other man's objections put you on the defensive. In one way or another, let all your words promote your cause.

Be An Approacher

"People are funny," a Los Angeles doctor remarked to me recently. "They will confidently go after everything they want —with one glaring exception. They hesitate going after new friends who can do them some good."

"How do you mean that?" I asked.

"When a man wants a haircut he heads straight for the barber; if he wants a new watch he marches directly to the jeweler. But far too often it is a different story when it comes to wanting new people in his life."

"Where do you think he goes wrong?"

"Well, everyone wants to think of himself as being wanted and needed by other people. Now, there's nothing wrong with that in itself. But people go wrong whenever they sit around and wait for evidence that they are wanted. They eagerly look for phone calls and letters and visitors. They are *waiters.* They wait for others to approach them."

"That's not good," I remarked. "It only builds up a damaging consciousness of being unwanted, of being left out. And *that* destroys self-assurance."

"Right. The whole problem revolves around this poor business of waiting for a sign that one is needed and necessary. Too many people think, 'If the other person will only surprise me with a phone call I'll be glad to return the favor.' They don't realize that the other person is thinking the very same thing. Someone has to have the courage to break the stalemate. The one who does so will change things dramatically. People are delighted with the person who takes the initiative in the making of or the furthering of a friendship. They usually show their appreciation by returning the friendly gesture."

One of the problems faced by President Lincoln during the Civil War was the timidly conservative attitude of some of his generals and political advisors. So fearful were they of a sudden sweep northward by the Confederate armies that they insisted on unreasonable defenses of Washington, D. C. That obsessive viewpoint, Lincoln realized, could only be held at the cost of winning the war by aggressive action. One of the over-cautious military men was General George Brinton McClellan, a soldier whose over-active imagination always saw the enemy troops triple in number to his own—even when the reverse was the case. The President, utterly weary of McClellan's idleness, sent him a telegram emphatically pointing out that an enemy army cannot be defeated by merely sitting and glaring at it.   Lincoln made it clear that the resources of the nation had been built to be thrown into bold and aggressive action against the enemy.

As it turned out, it finally took the firm forwardness of General U. S. Grant to bring victory to the North.

The lesson? Be an Approacher. Every way you can as often as you can. Devise new ways to meet new people. You don't have to think of clever ways to do it; simply do it. Walk on over and say *hello* just to see what happens. If you are unknown to the other person, so what? Everyone you now know was once unknown to you. There are no strangers; only friends you have not yet met. Dare to be the one who breaks the ice. This is how you start attracting those good people and rich relationships you need.

Especially never mind whether or not the other person seems approachable. It is the shy and distant people who appreciate your advance most of all. Never mind if they don't invite you; invite yourself. This isn't brashness; it's commonsense courage and a sure way to boom your self-confidence sky-high.

Besides all this, your advance toward the other person is just about the highest compliment you could pay him. He appreciates your forward movement, for it tells him, "Whoever you are, I like you."

Remember, everyone is instantly attracted to the person who dares to make the first friendly move. The Approacher gives us a glimpse of the superior person we could become. As Dr. Sidney M. Jourard writes in his book *Personal Adjustment*, "If we see someone doing something which we wish we had the moral fortitude to do ourselves, we admire them for the exemplary deed."[32]

---

32 Sidney M. Jourard, *Personal Adjustment* (New York: The Macmillan Company, 1958). Reprinted by permission of the publisher.

Since almost everyone mistakenly believes that the world in which he lives is the only world that exists, the daring personality hints to us of the brighter world which we might also find. The Approacher delights us when he frees us ever so slightly from the chains of fear and frustration.

A man once told me, "No sense kidding myself. I really am pretty shy when it comes to other people. As long as I'm that afraid I'll never make a resounding success of my life. I hope for the day when I get over it."

I told him, "I hope for the day when you get so sick and tired of being afraid of people that you make up your mind once and for all to find the solution which surely exists."

When two shy people meet, something rarely happens. When a shy and a confident person meet, something sometimes happens. When two confident people meet, something always happens. Do your part!

As a next move, let's discover one way in which you can make your approaches pay profits.

There was the clergyman who arrived home an hour late for dinner, to have his wife ask, "What kept you, dear?"

"Well," he replied, "you know Mrs. Green?"

"Yes."

"She has a slight cold."

"Yes."

"Well, I stopped long enough to ask her how she was feeling."

"And?"

"She told me."

You can always expect eager cooperation from others when you ask them to tell you about themselves. And while they are talking you should be listening. The idea is to let the other man himself tell you know he can best be turned into a friend or customer or helper. If you will listen carefully he will tell you every time. Do things the easy way. Let him tell you what he wants and needs. Now you can intelligently proceed to win him over by satisfying those desires.

This is how intelligence agents extract valuable information from captured enemy soldiers. They encourage their prisoners to talk about themselves, about their home towns, about their favorite foods and their plans for after the war, about anything at all. The agents know that a freely flowing tongue has a way of trickling through with valuable information, even when the prisoner is aware that his captors are after something. A captured German pilot of World War II was encouraged by his Allied guards to chat about his fishing experiences. The prisoner casually mentioned his luck while fishing in a certain Italian lake. From that clue his captors deduced that the pilot had come from a German airbase near that lake. Two days later an Allied bombing raid left the enemy base a wreck.

Make it your habit to encourage others to talk. You listen. Put your information to practical use for mutual benefit.

Summary of this section: Expand your influence over people by being an Approacher. Make full use of your contacts. "Be bold, be bold, and everywhere be bold." (Edmund Spenser)

Good Business for You

The fable is told of the powerful African lion who felt the need for some dinner. Stalking in the grassy plains he spotted and ran after a lumbering zebra. When a deer crossed their path the lion abandoned the zebra and set out after the deer. A moment later a gazelle caught the lion's attention, so the king of beasts again changed directions to race after the new game.

In rapid turn, the fickle lion sped back and forth after a goat, then a lamb, and finally, hours later, ended up wearily pursuing a white-tailed rabbit. The bobbing bunny easily escaped this exhausted—and pretty unwise—king of beasts.

The moral is, even powerful kings need to pursue their game in a business-like manner. Such practical virtues as consistency, concentration, and stability should not be ignored by anyone who really means to satisfy his needs.

In this final section of the chapter, I want to encourage you to place your plans for winning people on a systematic basis. But I want to emphasize that this does *not* mean that you have to proceed grimly or with strain.   So many people mistakenly believe that a business-like approach means painful effort and struggle. Nothing could be less true. As a matter of fact, I have made it a point in previous pages to show you that the relaxed and even the light-hearted approach is by far the more productive one. "A cheerful spirit is one of the most valuable gifts ever bestowed . . ." (Aughey)

Mr. A. is an inconsistent student of human relations. Mr. B. is a business-like one. What is the difference in attitude in the two of them? This:

Mr. A. looks at a successful man and puzzledly asks, "I wonder why he was lucky enough to win all that good fortune?"

Mr. B. studies the same successful man and curiously inquires, "I wonder how I can also win all that good fortune?"

The whole idea is to concentrate your cheerful energies toward the sole goal of understanding human nature as a means of winning your way in the world. That is the most profitable business you could ever get into.

Let me tell you a story about one man who used the business-like approach to increase his sales volume.

A manager of a supermarket, who was an eager student of human behavior, decided to put his knowledge to work in a practical way. One of the lessons he had learned from his studies was that most people have a certain amount of hesitancy about buying luxury items. Having been taught from childhood to be economical and conservative in spending habits, many people feel somewhat guilty about splurging beyond the practical necessities of life. Even though these subconscious guilts were pointless and unnecessary, still they were there.

That manager asked himself some interesting questions: What would enable his customers to break through these fixed feelings? What would persuade them to buy items which mistakenly meant "luxury" in their minds? That was the problem. He started to think about persuasive words and phrases. In particular he ran through his mind various "permissive" words, that is, those words which would free shoppers from their conditioned guilts, which permitted them to feel at perfect liberty to buy whatever their fancies chose, with no regard as to whether they were "luxury" items.

He printed a large sign with a single word on it. The word was followed by an explosive-looking exclamation point. The sign was set over the counter displaying some of the higher-priced items, like imported Italian sausage.

The result? Astonishing and gratifying. Sales of these particular delicacies rose a rewarding 23%.

The sign? It invitingly called out:

LIVE!

All of us without exception want to live more fully, with greater freedom of action, with less mental restriction, with more zest and enthusiasm, with greater thrills and multiplied pleasures. We have the constant urge to break through and crash out. "The cry of the soul is for freedom." (J. G. Holland)

That is why that single word produced the desired result. Shoppers increased their purchase of those items because they had been given permission to choose and live a bit more richly.

Your business-like application of your knowledge of human behavior can reward you similarly. Choose your objective and let other people give it to you. If you are tired of turning in a circle and always the same dull circle, here is your freedom.

For Expanding Your Influence Rapidly

1. Spectacular changes will occur in your life if you will proceed with self-expansion-through-other people.

2. Think constantly in positive terms of growth and prosperity and enrichment. These are your rights which you should claim.

3. Become aware of your tendency to make contacts only within your known world. Decide to break through to refreshing experiences.

4. Every desire you have is matched by nature with a power for attaining it.

5. Employ the techniques offered in this chapter for empowering yourself through your daily speech.

6. Remember that your words, spoken and written, are inexhaustible forces for influencing others. "Speech is power: speech is to persuade, to convert, to compel."* (Ralph Waldo Emerson)

7. Go straight after what you want from other people. "Dare to act!" (Tibullus)

8. Read and review the rich rewards won by an Approacher. Next, be one!

9. Listen attentively. Other people will tell you what you need to know for winning them.

10. Place your people-persuading programs on a professional basis. Diligence is always a wonder-working force.

15

MIRACLE-MAKING FORCES TO CHANGE YOUR LIFE

The story is told of a king of ancient India who summoned to his castle all the wise men of his kingdom.

He told them, "To the one who performs the miracle I request shall be given whatsoever his heart desires."

"What miracle, O King," asked the wise men, "do you require?"

"I wish," the monarch declared, "to have my name written on the bottom of the sea. Even the lowly creatures who inhabit the waters must know and honor my name."

The king and his subjects climbed the stairs to the royal court-yard which overlooked the blue sea. "Write my name on the depths of the ocean," the king again declared, "and your wish is granted."

One by one the wise men shook their heads and drifted away, defeated by the baffling problem. Presently, only one of his majesty's subjects remained at his side. Turning to him, the king inquired, "And you, wise man, will you also leave me without a solution?"

For an answer, the wise man picked up a sea shell, wrote the king's name on it, and tossed it into the deep.

Let this story remind you that miracles of change and newness can happen to you.

Your Mind Can Cause Miracles to Happen

The greatest miracle-making force in the world is *your mind.* Without the mind causing things to happen, nothing ever happens in this world. That is why we need to examine the vast empire of the mind as it relates to your plans for winning your way.

Your mind contains attitudes. Your attitudes determine your actions. Your actions result in either victory or defeat. It is therefore vital that we discover just what kind of attitudes a man employs toward both himself and toward other people.

We are going to look at 40 false attitudes which cause failure and unhappiness. By becoming aware of them, we can clearly see their opposites, that is, the opposite affirmative attitudes which result in affirmative actions which spell success and happiness.

Never take the attitude:

1. That there is no answer to your problem.

2. That other people bar your way to success.

3. That you have to do things the hard way.

4. That you cannot change for the better.

5. That conflict is a permanent part of your life.

6. That you cannot win what you want.

7. That people will never seek you out.

8.   That you must despair over personal faults.

9.   That you cannot be free of the past.

10. That you need be afraid of people.

11. That no one can help you.

12. That confusion is a necessary condition.

13. That you need be a slave to worry.

14. That you cannot win financial abundance.

15. That you have no inner resources.

16. That you must sacrifice yourself to others.

17. That your sex life cannot be bettered.

18. That courage will never come.

19. That you will never find fun in life.

20. That you cannot influence others.

If you find yourself a victim of any of these mistaken viewpoints, do an about-face at once. This will face you in the refreshing direction that leads to a new life.

To continue, never believe:

21. That life is pointless.

22. That your hurts will never go away.

23. That people need irritate you.

24. That anxiety is necessary.

25. That you have no right to rebel.

26. That you cannot command additional respect.

27. That the future is hopeless.

28. That failure cannot be overcome.

29. That you will never meet valuable people.

30. That the opposite sex need be a problem.

31. That loneliness cannot be dissolved.

32. That personal authority is not for you.

33. That you need be a victim of circumstances.

34. That you have no right to ask of others.

35. That heartache must be endlessly endured.

36. That mistakes cannot be corrected.

37. That other people do not need you.

38. That it is too late for peace of mind.

39. That you cannot brighten your personality.

40. That you will never find what you desire.

Charles K., an accountant, once dropped in for help. He informed me that he was weighed down by a mass of negative attitudes toward people, including some of the 40 just covered. He concluded his story by sighing, "It's hopeless, Nothing can really be done to improve my relations with other people."

Over the years I have found that nothing awakens a negative person more than the simple question with which I replied to Charles. I asked him, "How do you know? You *say* it's hopeless, you *think* it is, you *feel* it is, but honestly, Charles, *how do you really know?*"

Charles said he didn't know, then added, "I'm like a man opening new doors all the time and finding nothing more than another prison cell. Nothing can be done."

"How do you know?"

He shrugged.

"Let me ask, Charles, that you listen with a receptive mind as we go into this. What you claim you 'know' is merely a condition of your mind. Because you are conscious only of hopelessness, you wrongly conclude that hopelessness is all that exists. You think that you 'know' that nothing can be done because your mind says so. But your mind is playing tricks on you. Stop 'knowing' so much. Cease to think that you are thinking accurately. Do this and it won't be long before you are thinking on the outside of your negative circle. You will know what it is to be joyously free."

We then went into some of the plans contained in this book, especially those found in Chapter 7. Charles is presently finding his own magic power for persuading and commanding people.

Another caller, Helen B., told me that she was bothered by the negative attitude listed at point 37. She felt that other people just didn't need her.

"There is a simple way to change your mind about that" I told her. "Get into action. Prove to yourself that others not only need you but need you deeply and constantly."

The technique Helen used can also be employed by you. You can experiment personally by doing the following: Go out and buy a surprise for someone you like, perhaps your spouse or child or friend. It need not be an expensive gift, perhaps a box of candy or a pretty trinket, some little thing like that. If the receiver is the lady in your life, get her aside, pat her affectionately on the shoulder, tell her that you have a special surprise for her alone. Watch her face light up at the mere announcement. Now give her the surprise. Watch the delight that your surprising act inspires. *Also be alertly aware of the power you have to make another react favorably to you.*

There are few human hearts so cold that they will not melt before the warmth of the unexpected favor. "Please surprise me" is a constant yearning in everyone's heart. It assures us that the giver is thinking of us and that he likes us enough to spend time in arranging the event. The delight of being surprised is what makes a birthday gift so much fun to open and it is what makes us tingle when we get an unexpected phone call from someone we love.

Surprise has considerable commercial value also. The businessman who incorporates it into his plans will find that it pays dividends. It is the appeal that makes children race for the package with the unknown toy inside and also the power that urges us to buy Chinese cookies with their little messages always promising us forthcoming good fortune.

All of this makes the element of surprise a powerful people-persuader. If you want to command another's attention or affection or buying impulses then you should take the initiative in surprising him. You will be happily surprised at its ability to build your command.

The important thing to remember is that other people need you far more than you may think. They need your company, your personality, your time, and especially your influence. The secret of successful command is to make yourself so valuable a person that they of themselves seek you out. This is something you can certainly do.

Be Understanding

People will beat a path to the door of the man or woman who genuinely understands them. So many people unhappily feel that they have no one they can talk to, not a friend in whom they can confide, no one around to whom they can tell their troubles. And their unhappy feeling is unfortunately so often based in fact—there never are enough truly understanding people to go around. Oh, yes, there are those who impatiently put up with them, who give them phony advice, who listen only long enough to come back with some problem of their own. There are also those who want to reform them, but people don't want to be reformed, they want to be understood and liked and comforted.

"I understand," is pure magic to the other person when spoken and meant by you.

You can develop your understanding of people by using the techniques in this book slanted for that special purpose. As we have seen all along in these pages, it is your insight into people that gives you a mature power to enrich both them and yourself.

Take the time when the other person complains of being too tired to go along with your plans. The understanding individual will realize from the start that a man almost never complains of tiredness when that condition results from good and old-fashioned hard physical labor. As a matter of fact, people enjoy this kind of weariness, for there is genuine satisfaction in the sleepy state which comes after hard work well done. People who chronically complain of weariness do so for reasons connected with their complaints or frustrations. Human beings get tired emotionally for two reasons: 1. From doing things they really don't want to do. 2. From not doing things they really want to do.

By understanding this, you could look around for ways to free such a weary person from his emotionally-constructed prison.

The other day a friend of mine phoned to tell me that he just didn't feel like making the effort to attend a business meeting of a certain club. "Don't forget," I reminded him, "the business will be short. The rest of the evening is purely social-lots of food and fun!"

He laughed, "Funny, but all of a sudden I'm not as tired!"

"I understand" are two of the kindest words you can ever speak to another person—and also two of the most appreciated words the other man can ever hear you speak.

Let's look at that magic power we call *empathy*.

Empathy, that wise ability to understand another person's thoughts and feelings and sensitivities, can be used to win that other person. I want to tell you an illustrative story about one man whose kindly empathy makes him liked, appreciated, and sought after.

This man is a Los Angeles minister who receives many calls from people needing his counsel. One afternoon, while lunching together, he told me of a habitual practice of his:

"Once my phone starts ringing I always answer it as soon as I can, after the first ring if possible. There is a definite psychological reason for this. You see, many callers are timid about getting in touch with me in the first place. They somehow feel as if they're bothering me. So once they dial my number they get nervous, and the longer the phone rings the shakier they get. By answering promptly I cut off that nervous tension. Although a caller may not be consciously aware of what has happened, the end of the ringing and the start of our conversation represents a real relief which he appreciates."

By practicing empathy in such small matters as this, that minister has earned the right to be liked and respected.

(Incidentally, watch yourself sometimes, especially when dialing a prominent person or whenever you want a favor from someone. You will see what that minister was talking about!)

There is no time when your empathy means more to the other person than when he is upset or jittery or anxious. And since people experience these painful states quite frequently, they are always on the lookout for someone who can ease the pressure a bit. Here is what Dr. Camilla M. Anderson writes about it:

. . . the conscious or unconscious goal of every person in every detail of his life is to maintain himself as free from anxiety as possible . . . Anxiety is a psychological pain that is so uncomfortable that everyone does his best to be free from it.[33]

Develop your empathy.

Cheerful News

During a class I was conducting, one of the ladies brought up the question, "Why do you place so much emphasis on what we should *be?* Why not spend more time telling us what to *do?* After all, it's what we do that finally counts."

"Because," I replied, "the most persuasive force you possess is what you *are.* Most people have a dim awareness that their outer actions are but extensions of their inner selves, but a total awareness of this fact will work miracles of transformation."

Everything that you do depends upon what you are. If you are strong inwardly, you will express that strength in acts and words. If you possess poised emotions, you will display that poise naturally and effortlessly when with others. If you are basically a peaceful person, you will have no problem living peacefully and, incidentally, quite appealingly with those who know you.

A cherry tree produces cherries with naturalness and with spontaneity because it *is* a cherry tree. It doesn't have to struggle, it merely blossoms forth with its own nature. Likewise, when we work first of all with our own natures, we blossom with wholesome and attractive personalities.

This is an excellent time to speak of something that will always be likeable. I'm speaking of that happy trait called cheerfulness. It is something anyone can have.

---

33 *Saints, Sinners and Psychiatry,* by Camilla M. Anderson, M.D. Paperback ed., The Durham Press, Portland, Ore., 1962.

Want to know the natural condition of your life? "Nature designed us to be of good cheer." (Douglas Jerrold)

Like to build your strength? "Wondrous is the strength of cheerfulness, altogether past calculation its powers of endurance." (Thomas Carlyle)

Want to be thought wise? "The most manifest sign of wisdom is continued cheerfulness." (Michel Montaigne)

Wish to increase your health? "Cheerfulness *is*, in the first place, the best promoter of health." (Joseph Addison)

Like to be an inspiration to other people? "You find yourself refreshed by the presence of cheerful people. Why not make earnest efforts to confer that pleasure on others?" (L. M. Child) How can you release more cheer into your life?

Enjoy people.

Simply enjoy people. Learn to put fun and pleasure into every area of your human relations. Anyone can do it. All you have to do is do it.

> I am thinking of a woman who possesses an outstandingly at-
> tractive personality. When I asked her the secret of her constant
> popularity, she replied, "Easy, really. At one time I made up my
> mind that I was simply going to enjoy people, regardless of who
> they are or what they are like. What a relief to my nerves and a
> thrill to my day! It's miraculous how a simple decision like that
> can uplift everything. All you have to do is make up your mind
> that you are not going to do anything with people but to enjoy
> them. Know what? That makes them enjoy *you!*"

This must have been what English author John Ruskin meant when he declared, "You were made for enjoyment, and the world is filled with things you will enjoy."

All you have **to** do is do it.

Simple Systems for Swift Success

We have just covered some lively ideas for making thought-power work in your behalf. Now let's look at the logical follow-up to thought:

Action. "Thought and action are the redeeming features of our lives." (Zimmermann)

In this section you will discover some exciting techniques for using everything you have absorbed from this book. They add the finishing touch to the good work you have been doing all along.

1. SET ASIDE A CLARITY HOUR

A man once remarked to me, "You know my chief problem in life? Confusion. Plain old mental confusion. I have no doubts but that I would live ten times as happily if I could just learn to think clearly."

That man was echoing a major problem of millions of people. Confusion is a chief enemy of successful human relations. That is why you are acting intelligently when you set aside a Clarity Hour. This should be a period devoted entirely to clearing up questions and confusions. It is delightfully startling how a man recovers his inner strengths once he clears away the jungles of doubts and perplexities.

During your Clarity Hour, try to discover just where you may be holding yourself back. One man found that he was spending entirely too much time just thinking about his goals instead of acting upon them. Lots of people make that mistake. They make mental notes that someday they will do this or that, and that is as far as it goes. Don't store up mental notes. Learn to get your inspirations into immediate action. Whenever you think about doing something, do something about it. Even a small act carries you forward.

Use your Clarity Hour to turn your mind toward creative action. Example: For every thought you think about ways to save money, you should give 10 thoughts to ways to earn more money. You don't become wealthy through saving what you have; you win your financial fortune by acquiring what you haven't.

2. EXAMINE YOUR SUCCESSES

One day a Southern California man named Rudolph Boysen was looking over his blackberry patch when he spotted something extraordinary. One of the plants was entirely different from the others. Boysen curiously studied the surprising result in his blackberry patch, then decided to cultivate it. A seedling from that plant produced the large, juicy, colorful berry which bears the name—the boysenberry.

The most exciting and rewarding kind of study you can make is the examination of your successes, large and small. Whenever you score a hit through your skillful handling of people, look it over with an enthusiastic determination to uncover its secrets. Ask yourself exactly how you carried it off. Become aware of what you did that made things happen as they did. What techniques were used? Where can you duplicate its success?

It is a peculiar fact about the human mind that it resists looking closely at a success it has brought about. We have the peculiar notion that if we pay too much attention to success it will fly away. We feel as if there is some magic involved that should not be tampered with. Not only that, but we are so elated over the happy result that we miss the really significant point— the *cause* of that gratifying outcome.

While you should certainly enjoy any success you have brought about, you should spend most of your time looking with curiosity at the *creative factors* involved, and work at producing more of them. Good outcomes are automatic once you set the right causes into action.

3. LET YOURSELF BE SUPPORTED BY SCIENTIFIC PRINCIPLES

You can't go wrong in using the techniques of this book. Just remember that you are working with solidly scientific principles governing human nature. In other words, *they work*. Whenever you run into a problem with other people, look around for the proper system to support your plans for persuasion. By doing this you will not fail to see changes and improvements in both yourself and in those people with whom you live and associate. Have confidence in this.

Take as an example a time when you are dealing with a person who doesn't seem to respond to your persuasions. It could be an employer whom you wish to influence in your favor, or perhaps you want to help your spouse or your children. You may be tempted to think that nothing can be done, that he or she cannot change his behavior. You may believe that human nature is fixed in a pattern that cannot be altered. But what is the truth about it? Do people really change? Can a man's attitude and behavior be influenced? Here is the fact of the matter:

> Many people have the idea that attitudes cannot be changed. This is a false concept. Probably the most hopeful aspect of the study of attitudes is the observation that attitudes can and do change.[2]

One scientific way to change attitudes is through the use of repetition. Notice how the advertisers repeat their sales messages over and over. They know that a man first pays attention to the message. Then he grows curious as to what is offered. His alert interest then takes over. His desire to own the product mounts. He may finally go out and buy it. This principle can be varied and employed in all your human relations.

Let yourself be supported by all the powers of persuasion. They work.

4. KEEP YOURSELF ENTHUSIASTIC

"Enthusiasm," says Ralph Waldo Emerson, "is the leaping lightning."

In the first chapter of this book you discovered six exciting reasons why you should strike out with lightning-like enthusiasm toward your goals with people. At this point I want to make an addition which shows you *how* to keep yourself excited.

Look at the Upward Wave:

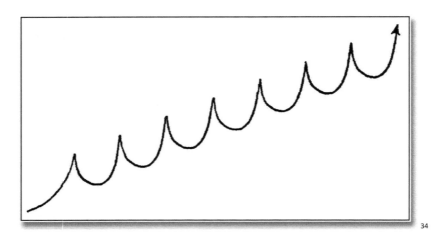

Any time you feel dismayed at your lack of progress in winning people, remember the Upward Wave. Picture it in your imagination. Let it remind you that no matter how pointless your journey *seems* to be, you are really traveling somewhere — *upward!* Even if you think that your plans have taken a downward dip, remember that it is *all part of the ever-rising Upward Wave.* Everything that happens to you with other people can be used as an elevating experience. Let it.

---

34 By permission from *Psychology in Business,* by Leslie R. Beach and Elon L. Clark, copyright 1959. McGraw-Hill Book Company, Inc.

Review Your Life-Changing Ideas

1. Remember the story of the king and the wise man, which opens this chapter. Let it encourage you to cause miracles to happen to your own life. Anyone can make miracles of change and newness.

2. Work at reversing the listed 40 negative attitudes. It is positively intelligent to examine and work with any negative attitudes you may find.

3. Never believe that confusion or hopelessness are necessary conditions in your life. If you only knew the freedom and peace that exists just beyond!

4. Believe that other people need you. They do.

5. Your understanding of the other person is a miracle-working force in your behalf. Everyone you know needs kindly understanding. Supply that need and they will seek you out constantly.

6. Develop your power of empathy. Learn to be aware of the other person's feelings and sensitivities. "You must look into people as well as at them." (Chesterfield)

7. Nature intends us to be cheery. Cheerfulness builds your energy. It is a sign of wisdom. It attracts and inspires others. It is easier to be cheery than gloomy. Reasons enough!

8. Decide that you are going to enjoy everyone you meet. Regardless of who or what they are, determine that you are going to get something of value from them. To do this is not selfishness; it is the height of intelligence.

9. Remember that the attitudes and opinions of other people can be changed. They can be changed by the persuader who works in harmony with the scientific principles of human nature. Let that influential scientist be you.

10. Keep the Upward Wave constantly before you in your imagination. It means that even your dips of doubt and discouragement are part of your upward progress. You have every reason to be enthusiastic toward your goals.

Chapter 16

SPECIAL SECRETS FOR YOUR PERSONAL PROGRESS

This chapter is your secret treasure chest!

We have been adventuring together in this book toward a single goal: The winning of your magic power to persuade and command people.

You now have knowledge of the techniques and procedures which make you skillful with people. To take those techniques and turn them into personal power — that is your next exciting adventure. It is the one that turns your hopes into realities — rich realities, such as greater personality-power and smoother interpersonal relations —a life occupied with peace and prosperity.

This chapter contains three special sections, all carefully designed to finally change your life into whatever you want it to be:

Section 1 is entitled My Secret Inspirations Found in This Book.

Section 2 is called My Secret Guidances for Winning Social Success.

Section 3 is headed My Secret Information for Daily Help.

Inspiration

Guidance

Information

These three treasures will guarantee your magic power to persuade and command people!

Section 1: My Secret Inspirations Found in This Book

At the very start of this book you were invited to share this secret section. For an exciting reason. As you read and review the various chapters you are bound to come upon certain ideas and sentences that strike you with special inspiration. They will thrill or impress you. They will arouse enthusiastic feelings. It is important that you retain and remember these significant discoveries.

So, as you read along in this book, be sure to jot down those techniques or pointers, those revelations or inspirations *which seem to apply especially to you and to your particular desires.* Somewhere in these chapters are just the right ideas for winning what you want. Make no mistake about that. This section will help you to remember and to organize these significant discoveries.

So, then, as you read and reread this book, turn to this section frequently. Here is how to fill in the following pages:

First, write down the page number where you found the exceptionally inspirational idea or plan. This locates it for you once and for all.

Second, write down the special secret itself. You need not use fancy language; just jot it down as simply and plainly as you like. For example, in Chapter 3 you will discover the exciting truth that it is just as necessary to learn how to *receive* as to know how to *give.* You might write it like this: "I must be constantly open and receptive to all the good things that other people have to offer me." As another for-instance, in Chapter 11 you will find out that any earnest person can brighten his personality in an amazing fashion. That happy idea might be noted: "I am really capable of building a dynamically attractive personality."

Third, you are going to additionally inspire yourself by listing several rewarding outcomes of applying this special secret. You might remind yourself: "When I am open to all the good found in other people, I win their friendship and their cooperation." Or: "My brighter personality will attract everything I need. Among other things, it contributes to my popularity, it builds my persuasiveness, and it advances my business career."

Special Secret No. 1

_____

_____

Page: _____

What it is: _____

_____

_____

_____

What it will do for me: _____

_____

_____

_____

Special Secret No. 2

_____

_____

Page: _____

What it is: _____

_____

_____

_____

What it will do for me: _____

_____

_____

_____

Special Secret No. 3

_____

_____

Page: _____

What it is: _____

_____

_____

_____

What it will do for me: _____

_____

_____

_____

Special Secret No. 4

_____

_____

Page: _____

What it is: _____

_____

_____

_____

What it will do for me: _____

_____

_____

_____

Special Secret No. 5

_____

_____

Page: _____

What it is: _____

_____

_____

_____

What it will do for me: _____

_____

_____

_____

Special Secret No. 6

_____

_____

Page: _____

What it is: _____

_____

_____

_____

What it will do for me: _____

_____

_____

_____

Special Secret No. 7

_____

_____

Page: _____

What it is: _____

_____

_____

_____

What it will do for me: _____

_____

_____

_____

Special Secret No. 8

_____

_____

Page: _____

What it is: _____

_____

_____

_____

What it will do for me: _____

_____

_____

_____

Special Secret No. 9

_____

_____

Page: _____

What it is: _____

_____

_____

_____

What it will do for me: _____

_____

_____

_____

Special Secret No. 10

_____

_____

Page: _____

What it is: _____

_____

_____

What it will do for me: _____

_____

_____

_____

Section 2: My Secret Guidances for Winning Social Success

You want to get definite results from this book. That is why you are using it. This section places your continued efforts on a businesslike basis by guiding you toward practical results.

This section is called your *secret guidances* for the simple reason that you are entitled to have your own private goals and ambitions. You may, of course, wish to let others know of some of your plans, especially if this book is being used as a textbook for a group program. However, even then, every participant should have his own book and should keep at least part of his plans as his own personal secret. This has a way of increasing your individual forcefulness.

Here is how to use the following guidances:

The *first* step is to write down exactly what you want from your social relations. Do this in just a few words, such as, "I want more self-confidence in dealing with business clients," or, "I'd like to be more at ease with people." For additional suggestions, refer to the list of 40 goals found in Chapter 1.

Next, list three procedures found in this book which you will use for advancing toward your selected target. For instance, the technique of Reverse Reaction (in Chapter 10) will always add more harmony to your interpersonal relations. If your goal is to understand human nature better, you could recall the story of the Cardiff Giant (in Chapter 4) and write something like this: "Remember that people believe what they want and need to believe." Add the page number where your secret system is located. You now have three workable techniques which you can employ as often as possible.

As a *third* step, list your first resulting successes from using your techniques. After a reasonable time period of employment, write down what happened. You may have succeeded overwhelmingly, or perhaps you at least achieved a good start. Example: "I persuaded him to be a somewhat more considerate person."

Fourth, use the *Comment* lines to write down anything helpful that occurs to you. For instance, you might remind yourself to use your three techniques for a two-week period, then replace them with three new ones. Or perhaps you might make a note of your determination to influence a certain person toward your way of thinking. One man of my acquaintance fires up his enthusiasm with notes like, "Things are really happening!" and, "Stick to it!"

Special Goal No. 1

What I want: _____

_____

Secret systems for winning it:

A. _____

B. _____

C. _____

Successes: _____

_____

_____

Comments: _____

_____

_____

Special Goal No. 2

What I want: _____

_____

Secret systems for winning it:

A. _____

B. _____

C. _____

Successes: _____

_____

_____

Comments: _____

_____

_____

Special Goal No. 3

What I want: _____

_____

Secret systems for winning it:

A. _____

B. _____

C. _____

Successes: _____

_____

_____

Comments: _____

_____

_____

Special Goal No. 4

What I want: _____

_____

Secret systems for winning it:

A. _____

B. _____

C. _____

Successes: _____

_____

_____

Comments: _____

_____

_____

Special Goal No. 5

What I want: _____

_____

Secret systems for winning it:

A. _____

B. _____

C. _____

Successes: _____

_____

_____

Comments: _____

_____

_____

Printed in Great Britain
by Amazon